DEATH
AND BURIAL IN
ANCIENT EGYPT

DEATH
AND BURIAL IN
ANCIENT EGYPT

SALIMA IKRAM

Longman

PEARSON EDUCATION LIMITED

Head Office:
Edinburgh Gate
Harlow CM20 2JE
Tel: +44 (0)1279 623623
Fax: +44 (0)1279 431059

London Office:
128 Long Acre
London WC2E 9AN
Tel: +44 (0)20 7447 2000
Fax: +44 (0)20 7447 2170
Website: www.history-minds.com

First published in Great Britain in 2003

© Pearson Education Limited 2003

The right of Salima Ikram to be identified as Author
of this Work has been asserted by her in accordance
with the Copyright, Designs and Patents Act 1988.

ISBN 0 582 77216 8

British Library Cataloguing in Publication Data
A CIP catalogue record for this book can be obtained from the British Library

Library of Congress Cataloging in Publication Data
A CIP catalog record for this book can be obtained from the Library of Congress

10 9 8 7 6 5 4 3 2 1

Typeset by Fakenham Photosetting Limited, Fakenham, Norfolk
Printed and bound in China

The Publishers' policy is to use paper manufactured from sustainable forests.

All photographs by the Author, except where otherwise stated.

TABLE OF CONTENTS

To Nicholas,
for surviving so many deadly drafts and moulting mummies.

ACKNOWLEDGEMENTS

I would like to thank Aidan Dodson, Nicholas Warner, Violaine Chauvet and John Swanson for their discussions, suggestions and comments. The indexing would never have been completed without the help of Peter Fiske and Roxie Walker. Without these, this book would not have been completed. I would also like to thank Heather McCallum for asking me to write it in the first place.

Introduction

Judging by the numbers of tombs and mummies that the ancient Egyptians left behind, one can be forgiven for thinking that they were obsessed by death. However, this is not so. The Egyptians were obsessed by life and its continuation, rather than by a morbid fascination with death. The tombs, mortuary temples and mummies that they produced were a celebration of life and a means of continuing it for eternity.

Death and birth are the two events universally experienced, and it is their very commonality that helps to link cultures, regardless of any separation in time or place. For the Egyptians, as for other cultures, death was part of the journey of life, with death marking a transition or transformation after which life continued in another form, the spiritual rather than the corporeal.

It is these tombs, temples and human remains that provide an insight not only into the religion and funerary beliefs of the ancient Egyptians but also into their daily life, economy and mastery of different technologies. Tombs and their contents are among the earliest types of remains that are preserved from ancient Egypt, and among the richest, hence the attention that has been paid to them by archaeologists.

The pyramids of Giza are situated in the desert beyond the fertile flood plain. Giza.

This book aims to provide a general understanding of the ancient Egyptian's funerary beliefs, customs and their physical expression, and thus an understanding of ancient Egyptian culture. One should be cautious, however, when interpreting the funerary culture of the ancient Egyptians, and remember that all that is believed by Egyptologists is merely an amalgamation of subjective interpretations with an imperfect data set. We are separated from the ancient Egyptians by time and by culture. The Egyptians did not leave any clearly written explanations of their beliefs and traditions, and what is presented in this book is the analysis of the available data by Egyptologists and, as such, is merely one interpretation of the funerary beliefs of the ancient Egyptians.

Salima Ikram
Cairo, 2002

1
The history and land of Egypt

The history of ancient Egypt is divided into dynasties and kingdoms (see Chronology). This division into dynasties is a result of the work of an Egyptian historian and priest, Manetho, a native of Sebennytos in the Delta, who lived in *c.* 280 BC. He was commissioned by the first Ptolemaic kings (Ptolemy I and II) to write a history of Egypt, with the ultimate aim that the Ptolemaic dynasty be linked to Egypt's earliest pharaohs and thus be seen as legitimate by the Egyptians. Using sources stored in temples, among other things, Manetho divided his history into thirty dynasties, to which later editors added one more, ending in 332 BC and the conquest of Egypt by Alexander the Great. Unfortunately, no complete copy of Manetho's history has been found, although portions have been preserved in the writings of later scholars who quoted Manetho extensively. Manetho's dynastic divisions are unusual as the dynasties do not end with the extinction of one family and begin with a new family. Instead, there are instances of more than one family ruling sequentially during the course of a dynasty, as well as examples of the same family ruling for two dynasties, with an inexplicable break of dynasties between the rule of a father and son.

The king-list in the temple to Osiris at Abydos built by Seti I is one of the most important historical documents from ancient Egypt. It provides a list of rulers from the earliest times until the reign of Seti. Abydos, photograph by J. Baines.

To augment the information left by Manetho, Egyptologists use other more ancient "king-lists" to better understand Egypt's sequence of rulers. "King-lists", as the name would suggest, are lists of kings that are found listed in sequence. However, they are not always straightforward or entirely dependable lists as they are a mixture of divinities who were supposed to have ruled Egypt during its "Golden Age" and revered ancestors, placed in a chronological order. These lists are found in different contexts: various temples (e.g. at Abydos and Karnak), annals detailing each year of a ruler's reign and one papyrus reference list. These lists help in understanding the history of Egypt, but they must be evaluated carefully as many are damaged and incomplete, while others were written to serve a specific political or religious purpose: to provide legitimacy of rule for a certain family or to discredit another ruler or family. In short, they only included kings that the compiler considered "legitimate". In order to obtain a more complete view of ancient Egyptian history, scholars also use carbon-14 dating, fixed astronomical dates, synchronisms with events in other Near Eastern countries and the archaeological record.

The division of Egyptian history into the Old, Middle and New Kingdoms is a construct of Egyptologists. Kingdoms, comprising groups of dynasties, are continuous periods of time with a stable central government ruling over a united Egypt. These are interrupted by Intermediate periods, characterized by no stable central government, and often with several dynasties ruling large areas independently. The history of a unified Egypt is preceded by the Predynastic and pre-historic periods.

Unification and the establishment of the Egyptian state

Prior to *c.* 3050 BC Egypt was not a unified country: the Nile valley was divided into what might loosely be called city-states with local rulers and divinities. This era is termed the Predynastic period, as it presaged the dynasties that would unite Egypt and rule for approximately 3000 years (see Chronology). There are distinct differences in the cultures of these different areas, especially between Upper Egypt (the south) and Lower Egypt (the north, mainly the Delta). The material culture that differentiates these cultures takes its form in pottery types, stone tools, houses and burial practices, including the location and shape of the grave, the body position and the grave goods included in the tomb.

The Predynastic period is divided into five main sub-periods, some of which are contemporary, each named after an archaeological site that produced the physical remains that are regarded as characteristic for each culture and period. In Lower Egypt, the Maadi culture was prevalent from *c.* 4000 to *c.* 3200 BC. In Upper Egypt the Predynastic is divided into three periods: the Badarian (*c.* 4500–4000 BC), followed by the Amratian or

Naqada I period (*c.* 4000–3500 BC), followed by the Gerzean or Naqada II period (*c.* 3500–3200 BC). Evidence for some presence of the Naqada culture in the north of Egypt starts during this time. From *c.* 3200 until *c.* 3000 BC the Naqada culture came to dominate the entire country, with its material remains found throughout Egypt and into southern Palestine. This time is known as the Naqada III/Dynasty 0 period and is the time during which the foundations of the Egyptian state were laid and the country was unified under King Narmer.[1]

The Early Dynastic period, also known as the Archaic period (Dynasties I and II), was a formative period of Egyptian history when the basics of the Egyptian bureaucratic state, art, architecture and religion were established. Royal cemeteries were established at Abydos and later at Saqqara. Non-royal cemeteries grew up throughout Egypt, with tombs belonging to more important officials clustering around Abydos and in the Memphite necropoleis (Giza to Saqqara). The start of an organized and literate bureaucracy is evidenced by the organization required to build and maintain the elaborate royal funerary places, and social differences are clearly illustrated by the different non-royal burials.

The Pyramid Age

The Old Kingdom (Dynasties III–VI) was a very stable and extremely prosperous period of Egyptian history, with a strong central government. Power was securely concentrated in the hands of the king who was regarded as a manifestation of the god Horus on earth and was worshipped as such. At no other time in Egyptian history was the king as powerful and authoritative. The well-organized bureaucracy of this period helped to facilitate the construction of the structures that give this period its soubriquet, the "Pyramid Age". During this time royal pyramids were constructed in the Memphite area, where the capital was located, with tombs of the high nobility clustered around them. To some extent the layout of the cemeteries reflected social hierarchy, as

Social organization is reflected in pyramid cemeteries: the king's pyramid is at the centre, with the mastabas of his family and court clustering around. Giza.

can be seen by the titularies of the nobles. During this time Egypt not only focused on its growth within the confines of the Nile valley but also controlled the oases and traded and fought against its neighbours in Libya, Nubia and the Near East.

The stability of the Old Kingdom did not last beyond the Sixth Dynasty. Then, because of an old and weakened ruler toward the end of the Dynasty, climatic changes that affected agriculture adversely and the growing power of various priesthoods and nobles, the government broke down and the land fell into disorder. The period from Dynasty VII (whose existence has recently been called into question by scholars) until the middle of Dynasty XI is called the First Intermediate Period. During this time there was no strong central authority; rather, the country once again broke into a series of warring city-states, all with different centres of power. From these different groups, two major powers emerged: Herakleopolis in the north, near the Fayum, and Thebes in the south, in the area of modern day Luxor. These two powers maintained an uneasy coexistence for some time, before engaging in a series of battles, with the Theban rulers emerging triumphant and reunifying the country.

This red granite statue of Senusert III shows the tired, woebegone expression commonly found in depictions of rulers of the late Twelfth Dynasty. Luxor Museum.

The Middle Kingdom and Second Intermediate Period

Mentuhotep II, the pharaoh responsible for reunifying Egypt, was the first pharaoh of the Middle Kingdom (Dynasties mid-XI–XIII). The Middle Kingdom saw a period of renewed prosperity for Egypt, with borders being extended to the south in Nubia, where enormous mud-brick fortifications were constructed, trade with the Near East being increased and remarkable strides being made in the fields of literature and medicine.

However, the pharaohs, although theoretically still god-kings, had lost some of the power and privilege that they had enjoyed in

Horses and chariots became an integral part of royal life after their introduction in the Hyksos Period. Metropolitan Museum of Art.

the Old Kingdom. Depictions of some of the later pharaohs show them with careworn faces, wearing protective amulets. This is in marked contrast to royal images from the Old Kingdom when the king is shown as youthful, virile and unconcerned. The Old Kingdom pharaohs certainly had no need for protective amulets as they were divine themselves. Religious privileges, such as funerary texts, accorded to the king in the Old Kingdom were now usurped by non-royal individuals: another indication of the king's decreased divine status. During the Middle Kingdom pyramids continued to be built for royal burials but, for the most part, they were poorly constructed and significantly smaller than those built during the Old Kingdom. The pyramids of this period are constructed primarily in the Fayum, which the Twelfth Dynasty developed agriculturally, and to the south of Memphis, near the new capital of Itj-Tawy, close to modern-day Lisht. Important officials continued to be buried around the king whom they had served, but to a lesser extent than in the Old Kingdom. Provincial burials on a fairly impressive scale at sites such as Beni Hasan,

Asyut, and Meir became common, and there was a considerable increase in the popularity of the god of the dead, Osiris.

The end of the Thirteenth Dynasty marked the close of the Middle Kingdom, with a series of weak rulers, an increase of power among the nobility and, most significantly, the arrival of the Hyksos. The Second Intermediate Period (Dynasties XIV–XVII) is the first time in the history of unified Eygpt that foreigners ruled a part of the country.

The term Hyksos comes from a corruption of the Egyptian term "heka khaswt", or rulers of foreign lands. Egyptian records of later periods, notably the Eighteenth Dynasty, characterize the Hyksos as fierce warriors who descended on Egypt from the Near East, pillaging and destroying the country, and ultimately controlling the north from their capital at Avaris, modern Tell el-Daba. Some research has suggested that perhaps the Egyptian description of the Hyksos may have been somewhat exaggerated and that the Hyksos were not as violent as they have been made out to be. On the other hand, other recent researchers have endorsed the older view of the belligerent invaders. They certainly were adept at warfare, introducing the horse, chariot and compound bow to Egypt, together with other new weapons. However, they soon adapted to Egyptian customs, traditions and religion and, to a large extent, were absorbed into Egyptian culture. While the Hyksos ruled the north, an Egyptian dynasty ruled in the south from Thebes. The Theban and Hyksos rulers clashed in battle several times. Ultimately the Thebans were victorious, and the Hyksos were expelled from Egypt.

Egypt's empire: the New Kingdom

Egypt was reunited in the Eighteenth Dynasty, marking the start of the New Kingdom (Dynasties XVIII–XX), with the capital being initially located at Thebes before being moved back to Memphis. From then on Thebes became the religious centre of the country, with Memphis acting as the administrative centre.

Perhaps as a response to the Hyksos domination, the Eighteenth Dynasty was a period of aggressive expansion to the north and the south on the part of the Egyptians. During this time Egypt extended its borders to the Fourth Cataract in the south and conquered large parts of the Near East, especially in the area of the Euphrates. Egypt became increasingly wealthy as a result of the resulting tribute and trade. Evidence of this can be seen in the art and material culture of this time. Much of the wealth accrued by the pharaohs was spent in the construction of temples; this is the time when most of the great temple of Karnak, dedicated to the chief god Amun, was constructed. The temple was continuously enlarged and enhanced throughout the New Kingdom and even thereafter. However, during the course of the Eighteenth Dynasty, in the reign of Amenhotep III, the pharaoh may have come to believe that the temple and priests of Amun had too much wealth and power, with the potential of challenging the sovereignty of the pharaoh. This laid the foundation for the religious and political upheaval known as the Amarna Revolution.

The Amarna Period is known for a shift in religious beliefs. It started slowly under Amenhotep III, but was carried to an extreme during the reign of his son, Amenhotep IV. During the course of his reign, Amenhotep III had started to distance himself from the cult and priesthood of Amun-re and to begin to focus royal favour on other divinities, especially solar divinities, with whom he directly associated himself. This perhaps harkened back to the Old Kingdom when the pharaoh was most closely identified with the sun god, Re. As part of this shift, he also resurrected the cult of a little-worshipped sun god, the Aten. Although the Aten was initially shown as a falcon-headed man, it soon became unique among Egyptian gods in being depicted neither anthropomorphically nor zoomorphically but, rather, as a sun-disc from which rays emanate. The only surviving anthropomorphic element is that the rays end in hands.

Amenhotep IV took the cult of Aten to an extreme, perhaps through religious as well as political convictions. He changed his own name

Akhenaten and Nefertiti oblating to the Aten who stretches out his rays ending in hands toward the royal couple, offering them life in return. Cairo Museum.

to Akhenaten (the living spirit of the Aten), apparently closed down the temples to Amun (and Osiris), and moved the capital to a hitherto unoccupied site in Middle Egypt, modern el-Amarna, ancient Akhetaten (the horizon of the Aten). Akhenaten lived and reigned from here, where the cult of the sun and the cult of the pharaoh as the son of the sun flourished. The art of this period shows Akhenaten and his family as unusually shaped individuals with elongated heads, slanted eyes, loosely hanging bellies and large hips. Perhaps the pharaoh used such depictions to separate himself and his family, who were viewed as divine, from all other people, who were not divine, during this period. However, the courtiers were also depicted in a manner similar to that of the king, perhaps as a form of flattery.

King Ramesses III, armed with a bow and arrow, and mounted on his chariot, advances against the enemy which falls in confusion before his attack. Karnak.

Little is currently known about what happened in the rest of the country during this time. Akhenaten has been accused of ignoring the outer reaches of Egypt's empire, although this has been disputed. However, it is clear that in Egypt the new religion and its advocate, the pharaoh, had little support among the courtiers and people. The Amarna period lasted less than twenty years. Akhenaten and his immediate successors, including Tutankhamun, are deleted from many subsequent king lists, despite the fact that his successors restored the cult of Amun, leaving the cult of the Aten to sink, once again, into obscurity.

In the Nineteenth Dynasty the dynamic ruler, Ramesses II, appears to have moved the capital to the eastern Delta, to the site of Pi-Ramesses, modern Qantir. Thebes retained its eminence as a religious centre. Egypt maintained its prosperity throughout this period with military actions being carried out against the Hittites, Libyans and Nubians. Trade relations also flourished despite the warfare, and luxury goods poured into Egypt. The Twentieth Dynasty, however, saw a radical change in Egypt's

fate. Egypt was repeatedly attacked by the Sea People, a loose affiliation of peoples from the eastern Mediterranean. Ramesses III managed to withstand their attacks for some time, but, ultimately, his successors, a series of weak kings, lost control of the country, leading to its disintegration.

Twilight of Egyptian history

The Third Intermediate Period (Dynasties XXI–XXV) was a period of political fragmentation and civil unrest. A large influx of foreigners not only moved into Egypt but also ruled the country. The Twenty-second Dynasty was of Libyan origin, and the Twenty-fifth Dynasty was Nubian. The foreign rulers, for the most part, were thoroughly Egyptianized: they worshipped Egyptian divinities, spoke and wrote Egyptian, and upheld Egyptian traditions and beliefs, as well as continuing its bureaucracy and administration. Thus, Egypt maintained its cultural integrity.

The capital of Egypt moved around throughout this period, with Tanis (where the kings of the Twenty-first and Twenty-second

Dynasty were buried) and Thebes being the two main locations. Thebes maintained its religious ascendancy throughout this period, although Tanis acted as the Thebes of the north. Even the temples of Tanis were organized in such a way as to mirror the arrangement of the Theban temples. During this time, the cult of Amun remained much in evidence: new temples to the god were inaugurated and older ones augmented. The rulers of the Twenty-fifth Dynasty eventually retreated to Nubia as a result of repeated military engagements with the Assyrians who were trying to dominate Egypt. Ultimately, the Assyrians themselves were expelled from Egypt, and the country was once again ruled by an Egyptian king in the Twenty-sixth Dynasty.

The Late Period comprises Dynasties XXVI–XXX. The Twenty-sixth Dynasty, with its capital at Sais, saw a re-establishment of Egypt's prosperity, its art and architecture. The archaism in the art of the period is extremely interesting, as it harkens back stylistically to the art produced during the Middle and New Kingdoms.

The Twenty-sixth Dynasty had managed to achieve its victory against the Assyrians by using foreign mercenaries, many of whom settled in Egypt. In the Late Period Egypt's population was extremely diverse with Nubians, Libyans, Greeks, Carians, Assyrians and other people from the Near East settling in Egypt. In 525 BC the Persian ruler, Cambyses, invaded and established the Twenty-seventh Dynasty, with Egypt as a province of the Persian Empire. The Persians were never popular rulers, despite their early additions to temples and other buildings in Egypt, and the Egyptians kept fomenting unrest. In 404 BC Amyrataios of Sais gathered together an army and managed to expel the Persians, thus returning Egypt to Egyptian rule. His dynasty was quickly replaced by another Egyptian dynasty, based in Mendes, which in turn was displaced by the last Egyptian dynasty, the Thirtieth Dynasty. The Persians regained control of Egypt in 343 BC.

The temple to Hathor at Dendera was built by the Ptolemies. The only confirmed large-scale representation of Cleopatra VII, the last Egyptian ruler, is on the rear wall of this temple. Dendera.

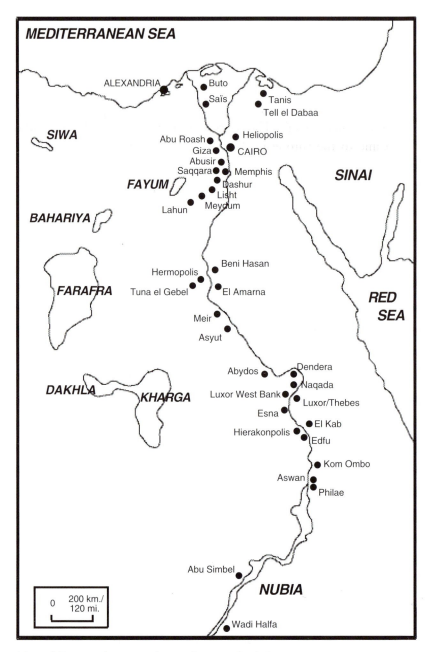

Map of Egypt with principal sites. Drawing by J. Swanson.

Persian control of Egypt came to an end with Alexander the Great's conquest of Egypt and the Persians in 332 BC. Alexander was hailed as a god by the enthusiastic Egyptians, who were relieved to be finally free of Persian oppression. Egypt was part of Alexander's Hellenistic Empire for only a short while. On the untimely demise of Alexander in 323 BC, his empire was divided among his generals. The control of Egypt passed to Ptolemy, who came to the throne in 305 BC. Prior to that, Egypt had been ruled by Alexander's half-brother, Philip Arrhidaeus, and his son, Alexander IV.

Ptolemy I, a Macedonian, founded the Ptolemaic Dynasty that ruled Egypt from Alexandria until 30 BC. Ptolemy I worked to unify the disparate populations resident in Egypt, primarily Greeks and Egyptians, through various governmental and religious policies. However, his successors seemed to be less successful at blending the two groups and lived at a remove from their Egyptian subjects, ignorant to a large extent of their culture and language. A notable exception to this was Cleopatra VII, the last of the Ptolemies, who was well versed in the religion and language of ancient Egypt. It was during her reign that Egypt, enfeebled by generations of royal power struggles, eventually fell to the Romans and became a province of Rome in 30 BC. However, even though Egypt itself had ceased to exist as an independent political entity, Egyptian culture, notably its religion and funerary beliefs, continued to flourish and was adapted, adopted and exported by the Romans so that elements of Egyptian religion permeated throughout the Empire. Thus Egypt enjoyed a certain culturo-religious victory over the Romans.

Climate and topography

Egypt is physically divided into two: Lower Egypt, or the Delta and the areas north of modern Beni Suef, and Upper Egypt, the south. The two portions take their names from the direction of the flow of the Nile, from south (thus upper) to north (lower).

These two portions of the country are called the Two Lands, and one of the titles of pharaoh who ruled over the united country was Lord of the Two Lands. Each land was associated with a plant and an animal. The north was associated with papyrus and a cobra (an incarnation of the goddess *Wadjet*), and the south with the lotus and a vulture (a manifestation of the goddess *Nekhbet*). Each half of the country had a crown, with the red crown generally regarded as belonging to Lower Egypt, and the white crown to Upper Egypt.

Generally when one thinks of Egypt one thinks of the Nile Valley and Delta as constituting the only habitable part of the country. However, during the Predynastic period the Egyptian climate was much wetter than it is today. The Delta was extremely marshy. Settlements were located on portions of dry land that emerged from the water called turtle-backs. The area to the south of the Delta is characterized by a valley and cliffs that have been carved out of a plateau by the activity of the Nile and its grander predecessor, the giant Ur-Nile. A floodplain borders the river itself, petering out into the desert, with cliffs rising up beyond. Through the valley, the width of the floodplain varies greatly, from a metre or two to several kilometres.

Settlements were located not only along the Nile, at the edge of the floodplain, but in areas that are now deserts, which were once filled with vegetation and water sources. The oases are also areas where Egyptian towns and settlements of significant size were located. The settlements in the Nile Valley tend to be located out of the reach of the Nile flood. The flood, due to rains in the highlands of Ethiopia and Uganda, augmented by the flow of the Atbara River in modern Sudan, was formerly first noticeable in Aswan by the end of June, reaching its full height by September. During this time most of the cultivatable land would be below water, and it is thought that it is during the flood that peasants and others were drafted into providing the unskilled labour (perhaps as part of a corvée system) for building projects, such as pyramid construction, as they were not needed on the farms.

The Egyptian calendar was determined by the inundation,[2] and thus divided into three seasons. The first season, inundation, *Akhet*, was followed by the going forth of the waters and the planting season, *Peret*, with the final season being the time of harvest and relative drought, *Shemmu*. The inundation deposited rich silts on the fields and washed away any salts, thus providing, when the floods were good, an absolutely ideal environment for high agricultural productivity. It is no wonder that the ancient Egyptians regarded their land as better than all others and had a tendency to believe in their own cultural superiority – no Egyptian wanted to die outside his country, and, in the case of such an unfortunate event, the body was brought back to Egypt for burial. Certainly all those who invaded or settled in the country were absorbed into Egyptian culture and adopted Egyptian ways. In some instances, the settlers exported Egyptian cultural practices, such as the cults of Isis and Osiris, back to their native lands (as was the case with the Romans).

The flora and fauna of Egypt were also more diverse during Egypt's earlier history, including lions, hippopotami, elephants, giraffes and many different sorts of antelope. It is only by the end of the Old Kingdom that the desert increased in area and water sources decreased, and the main areas of settlement retreated to the Nile valley and oases. Throughout Egyptian history the country's fauna gradually changed its character, partly because of climatic and environmental change as well as increases in human population, over-hunting and the introduction of new species.

The topography and environment of Egypt are also partially responsible for its culture and history. The Egyptian state and its culture were able to establish and maintain themselves to some extent owing to Egypt's natural boundaries. To the north Egypt is bordered by the Mediterranean Sea, which was unnavigable by the ships of earliest antiquity. Access to the Near East is through the easily controlled northern Sinai, an area that is now dry, but was once home to the Pelusiac branch of the Nile. To the south, the Nile River, the main "roadway" of Egypt, is impassable at the First Cataract, an extrusion of granite rocks that would smash any vessel to smithereens. Access to the south entails skirting of the river or taking remote and dangerous caravan routes in the Western desert. The eastern boundary is marked by the Red Sea. Thus, Egypt was, for the most part, well protected from exterior forces for the greater part of its history. This topographical protection might have been, in part, responsible for the conservatism of Egyptian culture. Once ideas and customs were established, there was a tendency to continue them, albeit with some changes and innovations over time.

To some extent one can say that culture is a reaction to one's environment. Certainly a large part of culture, whether physical or intellectual, is influenced by the environment. For example, on a practical level, secular and sacred buildings and architectural styles developed to meet the demands of climate, topography and available raw materials. Thus bundles of easily available papyrus that are used as pillars for domestic buildings are transformed into stone facsimiles that are used in temples. In the sacred context the papyrus columns had not only a practical but also a metaphorical role as flourishing, green papyrus plants that are symbolic of life and health. The Egyptian writing system, hieroglyphs, is derived from the images of the natural world that surrounded the Egyptians.

Religious beliefs are born to explain certain natural phenomena and are inspired by the natural world. One of the Egyptian creation myths, which explains how the first piece of land emerged from the primeval ocean of Nun, is based on the inundation. The first inhabitants, a group of gods and goddesses that were serpent and frog headed, reflect the animals that first emerge from the Nile mud. In Egyptian mythology, the night sky is transformed into the goddess Nut who stretches herself over the earth, personified by the god Geb, in her dark blue dress, decorated by twinkling stars. Thus, Egyptian religious beliefs justified the world around them, and, perhaps as the environment was stable, the beliefs and customs of the Egyptians maintained their stability and continuity as they satisfactorily explained the world in which they lived.

Notes

[1] The name of the pharaoh who unified Egypt is still disputed. Some scholars suggest Menes, while others opt for Narmer. Presumably unification took some time and was a result of the growing cultural hegemony of Upper Egypt. This might have been cemented by a series of battles between the northern and southern parts of the country, with the chief ruler of the south of Egypt being ultimately victorious over his northern counterpart.

[2] The flooding of the Nile Valley stopped completely in 1971 with the completion of the Aswan High Dam.

2
Beliefs in the Afterlife

The Egyptians saw Egypt as the most perfect land in the world, and the centre of the universe. According to them, their country's environment and natural and social orders were decreed and established by the gods. In order to maintain these, and to continue Egypt's physical and cultural existence, *maat*, or divine order, had to be maintained. It was the duty of every individual to contribute to maintaining the balance of the cosmos (*maat*), although the pharaoh and the priests bore most responsibility for this. By appeasing the gods through offerings and prayers, and by living within the laws of *maat*, life could continue in Egypt. To be Egyptian was to be of the best people, and to live and die in Egypt was the aspiration of every Egyptian. The tale of Sinuhe relates how Sinuhe returned to Egypt to die. In fact, if an Egyptian died abroad, all possible efforts were made to retrieve his body and bring it back to Egypt. There seems to have been a very real fear that, if one died outside the country, the Afterlife was not guaranteed. It is this belief that prompted the official Sabni (Dynasty VI) to embark on a hazardous trip through sub-Saharan Africa to retrieve the body of his father, Mekhu, and to bring it back to his home in Aswan for burial. Part of the Egyptians' concept of life was its

continuity after death in a more perfect celestial Egypt, also known as the Fields of Iaru. This, too, could be arranged by following *maat* and religious guidelines that would perpetuate the individuals' lives beyond death.

The majority of what is known of the Egyptians' belief of the Afterlife is derived from evidence dating to the New Kingdom and later. However, the basic ideas seem to have been in place from the dawn of Egyptian history and appear to have evolved during its course. Evidence of funerary goods from tombs of the Badarian period onward indicates a very early belief in life after death. The Egyptians believed that after their transitory life on earth they would move to a more permanent life in a place that was an enhanced Egypt. This place, which could be either subterranean and a mirror image of Egypt, or celestial, was often called the Fields of Iaru, or Field of Reeds, and was the domain of the god Osiris (see below). Here the deceased, as a *maa kheru*, or justified one, could live eternally at one with the gods.

Aspects of the individual

The physical body was crucial to a continued existence in the hereafter, especially as the *ka* and the *ba* (see below) needed to be periodically reunited with it if they were to survive. The body provided a link to the earth as well as to the offerings and magical texts inscribed on the tomb chapel's walls. The desire to protect and preserve the physical body is what probably gave rise to mummification (see Chapter 3). The mummified body was, to some extent, supposed to be more perfect and eternal than the body had been in life. In the Old Kingdom the body was preserved in such a way that it became an image of itself, a statue almost (in Egyptian, *twt*), while in later periods it was encased in cartonnage to produce a similar effect. Thus, it became a projection of the idealized and more permanent self. The words used to designate a living body, a corpse and a mummy are all different.

Ramesses IV (Dynasty XX) and the goddess Maat, wearing the feather of truth as her headdress. Valley of the Kings, photograph by J. Swanson.

A living body was usually termed *khet*, while a corpse was called *khat* and a mummy was called *sah*.

A person's heart was regarded as the most important part of the physical body, as this was where the soul, spirit, personality and very essence of an individual were supposed to reside. The heart figured prominently in the idea of resurrection. The heart remained in the body throughout mummification (see Chapter 3) and was protected by a very important amulet: the heart scarab. The heart, as the organ that identified an individual's "essence", was weighed on a scale against the feather of *maat*. If the heart and the feather were balanced, it meant that the person had led a good and just life. If it were heavier, then the person would forfeit the Afterlife and be consumed by Ammit (see below).

The Egyptians believed that, in addition to the physical body, a person was made up of different component parts that, when taken together, constituted an entire individual: *ren*, the name; *shuyet*, the shadow; *ka*, the double or life-force; *ba*, the personality or soul; *akh*, the spirit. A major part of Egyptian funerary religion is devoted to ensuring the survival of not only the body, but of all these components.

The name of an individual was one of the most important parts of personhood, in both this life and the next. A name provided one with an identity; without a name one was rendered a non-person, and would cease to exist, the worst possible fate imaginable. This is why the Egyptians went to extreme lengths to safeguard and perpetuate their names. Tombs had their owners' names and titles inscribed in several places, starting with the doorways, door-jambs, and moving inward. Visitors to tomb-chapels were encouraged to read aloud the tomb-owner's name so that, with each reading, he would be remembered and would continue to flourish in the Hereafter. Objects belonging to the tomb-owner were frequently inscribed with their name. Statues and two-dimensional representations of the deceased were similarly labelled so that the

This wooden statue of King Hor is known as a ka-statue because of the ka symbol on the head. This was probably a focal element in the celebration of his mortuary cult. Egyptian Museum, photograph by A. Dodson.

tomb-owner's name was preserved for eternity. These statues, in addition to the mummified body, also provided a vehicle for the animation by the *ka*, and were called *ka*-statues. In the Graeco-Roman period, when people were frequently buried in mass graves, mummy-labels bearing the name and title of the deceased were attached to the mummies, much like dog-tags, thereby ensuring their correct identification and continuation into the Afterlife. If the name of an individual was mutilated, hacked out or faded, the Egyptians feared for his eternal existence.

Thus, considerable attention was paid to ensuring that a person's name was securely attached to him through life and death. To render someone non-existent, one had to erase their name. Thus, the erasure of Akhenaten's name was a means of eradicating his existence from Egyptian history. Akhenaten himself tried to annihilate the god Amun by removing his name from all monuments and trying to negate his existence. This practice of *damnatio memorae* was judged as an effective means of forever removing the existence of any undesirable individual. For magical spells, knowing someone's name gave one power over that person. In one Egyptian myth, the goddess Isis gained power over the god Re by learning his secret name. This obsession with one's name is common to all people worldwide; one has only to look at graffiti from anywhere in the world to see people's need to leave some evidence of themselves behind by leaving what they consider was the essential manifestation of themselves: their name.

The shadow is described in funerary texts as a powerful and speedy entity that had to be protected. The word for shadow itself, *shuyet*, also suggests shade and protection, and in royal contexts the pharaoh is often shown being protected by a feather- or palm-fan. Both the feather and palm have metaphoric meanings in Egyptian religion; the feather is a symbol of *maat*, and indicates that whomever is shaded by it is protected by *maat* and will lead a good life, in both this world and the next. The rib, or central portion, of a palm frond leaf is the Egyptian word for year and might suggest a lengthy life. Naturally, shadows were also associated with the sun. This solar association was closely linked to the idea of an individual's rebirth: the sun produced a person's shadow, an image of the individual. When the sun left the sky, the shadow vanished, only to be reborn, with the help of the sun, on the following day. Thus, the sun would help the individual in all his forms to be re-produced for eternity in the Afterlife.

The idea of the *ka* is very complex and, like many Egyptian religious ideas, is still imperfectly understood. This very crucial aspect of the personality was created at the same time as the body and continued through life and into death, rather like a doppelganger or twin. It was the force that animated the individual.

There are several images showing the creation of a person on a potter's wheel by the god Khnum, who simultaneously created the person's *ka*. In some instances, funerary statues represent the individual beside his *ka*, or show the *ka* standing behind its double. Some *ka*-statues are differentiated from the people whose *ka* they represent by being crowned by the hieroglyphic sign for *ka*, a pair of upraised arms. These arms can be interpreted as indicative of protection from evil, praise or even of embracing, perhaps in a sexual context, since phonetically *ka* is linked to words associated with reproduction.

From the Old Kingdom onward texts suggest that the *ka* continued to live after the body's demise and required the same sustenance that the body had enjoyed during life. Another name for a tomb was "the house of the *ka*". The *ka* was the main recipient of the food offerings given to an individual after death. The offering formulae inscribed on tomb walls or on offering tables were directly addressed to the *ka* of the deceased, as without sustenance the *ka* and the deceased would not survive through eternity. The

Ankherkau in his ba bird form, at his tomb. The arms are raised in prayer. Photograph by J. Swanson.

ka did not consume the food, but absorbed the potential suste-nance that it provided, and was thereby fuelled for an active Afterlife. After a person's death, the *ka* seems to have been primarily restricted to the mummy itself, representations of the deceased and the burial chamber and tomb-chapel (see Chapter 6).

The *ba* was depicted as a human-headed bird, some-times shown with arms. This is the form in which the spirit travelled from the burial cham-ber up through the shaft to the tomb and cemetery. The *ba* was one of the most mobile aspects of the personality and appears to have been primarily manifested after the death of an individual, although certain texts relating to dreams suggest that during sleep (a state akin to death) the *ba* could be released to travel. This aspect of the personality had all the characteristics enjoyed by a human: an ability to eat, drink, speak, move and travel. The *ba* could travel in this world, the Afterworld or even with the sun god in his sacred barque. The depiction of the *ba* as a human-headed bird might be related to its phonetic kinship with the

Part of a curse formula from the tomb of Hesy (Dynasty VI) at Saqqara. The word akh, written with the crested ibis, appears three times.

Osiris enthroned in his kiosk, waiting to judge the dead. Abydos.

word for stork. This bird-like aspect of the *ba* enhanced its mobility, and the association of the deceased with migratory birds who go away and return (are reborn). Despite its ability to travel, the *ba* had to return to the physical body of the deceased in order to be reunited with its physical anchor, or the deceased would not survive. Many prayers and spells in various funerary books (see below) concern the reunion between the body and the *ba*. In *The Book of the Dead* Chapters 17 and 89 are particularly concerned with the merging of the *ba* with its mummy and are spoken over a statue of a *ba* bird that is placed on the breast of the deceased.

Both gods and humans possessed a *ba*, although the divine *ba* had more diverse characteristics than the human *ba*. The *ba* became increasingly important in funerary texts from the Middle Kingdom onward, although it was not generally depicted until the New Kingdom, when representations of the *ba* became common and remained popular until the end of the Roman period. The *ba* is shown in several different contexts: hovering over the deceased, while clutching in its talons the *shen* sign, symbol of eternity, at the tomb's doorway, in the shaft of the tomb, and clasped in the hand of the deceased. Coffins from the late Second Intermediate Period and the New Kingdom assume the form of the *ba*. During this time, anthropoid coffins, bearing the face of the deceased, with the entire body area decorated with a feathered pattern (*rishi* coffins), became popular. These coffins have been variously interpreted as a manifestation of the deceased's *ba* or an allusion to the protection offered to the deceased by the goddesses Isis and Nepthys.

Of all the different aspects of the personality, the concept of the *akh* is the most complicated and esoteric. The *akh* is thought to result from a union of the *ba* and the *ka*, which created the *akh*.

Predynastic tomb Uj was many chambered and made of mud brick. It is possible that the walls were originally hung with reed mats that were later copied in faience by Djoser in the subterranean portion of his pyramid. Abydos.

Thus, the *akh* was the deceased transfigured into an eternal and unchanging living being of light, frequently associated with the stars. Not everyone became an *akh*, as people who had lived lives that were not in harmony with *maat* would be annihilated. However, all funerary texts and rituals were directed toward a successful Afterlife and the creation of the *akh*.

The Egyptians wrote *akh* using the hieroglyphic sign of the Hermit or Bald Ibis, *Geronticus eremita*. This bird, now extinct in Egypt, is distinguished by a long neck, which, like the head, bill, legs and feet, is red. The head is surrounded by a striking ruff of bluish feathers. The body of the ibis is a very dark blue, with many of these birds having lighter blue and red patches on their wings. The redness of the head, coupled with the blue of the ruff, suggests aspects of the sun and the sky: red is a solar colour, and the ruff, especially when viewed frontally, suggests the rays of the sun. The birds' overall blue colour alludes to the sky. Thus, the celestial nature of the *akh* is underlined by the hieroglyph that represents it.

The *akh* was closely associated with the gods and shared some of their characteristics, although it was not truly divine itself. Other words associated and derived from *akh*, spirit, reflect this relationship. Some of these words can be translated as becoming glorious, splendid, beneficial, or are associated with the power of gods. The *akh* only came into being after the death of a person and symbolized a successful rebirth and resurrection: the person was transformed from being a mortal into an immortal. In the Old Kingdom the *akh* was primarily identified with gods and kings (divine in their own right), and only became more commonly identified with non-royal individuals thereafter.

Kings, especially in the earliest periods of Egyptian history, had a slightly different Afterlife from that of non-royal individuals. As kings were divine beings, they joined the other gods after death, and journeyed with the sun god through the skies and the underworld as part of his entourage. Their *akhu* (plural) were more divine than those of lesser mortals and shared in the divine power of the major gods.

The myth of Osiris

Funerary beliefs in ancient Egypt were, to a large extent, associated with the myth of the god Osiris. Depictions of Osiris became common until the Later Middle Kingdom. He is frequently represented as a mummiform individual, his arms crossed over his chest, with his hands clasping a crook and a flail. He is crowned with the *atef* crown, consisting of the white crown flanked with two plumes (an allusion to *maat* which is often denoted by a feather), sometimes with two curling horns emerging on either side of the crown, perhaps alluding to Khnum and his role as the creator of the physical body and the *ka*. The mummiform portion of his body is white, like mummy bandages, while his flesh is painted black or green. The black alludes to the rich fertile alluvial silt deposited by the Nile, while the green symbolizes the plants that grow in the soil. Both black and green were colours of rebirth and resurrection in ancient Egypt and were associated with the potential of the earth to bring forth life.

Although references to Osiris date back to the Old Kingdom, at least, there are no complete written records of the overall Osiris myth until the Greek period. The most coherent account is that of the Greek historian, Plutarch. However, it is probable that the myth evolved and changed shape over time, and that the Greek account is a modified version of the Egyptian original.

The story, as derived from the Egyptian and Greek sources, is briefly as follows. In the Golden Age of Egypt the gods ruled the world. The ruler of Egypt was Osiris, with Isis, Great of Magic, his wife and sister, ruling beside him. As the king, Osiris was identified with the physical land of Egypt. Thus the state of the land and fertility were associated with the regenerative forces of the king. This force is manifested in the *heb-sed* race and festival associated with divine kingship and the well-being of the country.

Osiris was a good and just ruler who aroused the jealousy of his brother Seth. Seth plotted to overthrow his brother and rule in his stead, so he conceived a nefarious plan. Seth discovered the measurements of his brother's body and had a richly decorated chest made to these measurements. He then planned a magnificent banquet to which he invited his seventy-two cohorts, as well as Osiris. Toward the end of the feast, when everyone had indulged sufficiently, he had the chest brought forward and offered it as a gift to anyone who could fit into it. Much as in the story of Cinderella, everyone tried to fit into the highly ornamented casket, but to no avail. Finally Osiris was persuaded to try it. Naturally he fitted perfectly. Seth slammed down the lid, locked the casket and sealed it with molten lead. Then this earliest of coffins, containing the body of Osiris, was flung into the Nile.

The casket was carried by the river's current into the Mediterranean Sea and thence to Byblos (in modern Lebanon). There it became lodged in a tree. Isis, mourning her husband's disappearance, went in search of him and eventually located him in Byblos. She brought Osiris in his casket back to Egypt. There, however, Seth, who had established himself in the interim as ruler of Egypt, found him, and, opening the box, removed Osiris and cut him into pieces that he scattered throughout Egypt. The number of pieces into which his body was divided varies from fourteen to forty-two (the latter being the traditional number of *nomes* or provinces of Egypt).

Isis, together with her sister Nepthys who was married to Seth, went in search of Osiris's body-parts. She gathered these together and reassembled her husband's corpse. One very crucial portion of his body was not to be found: Osiris's phallus had been eaten by a fish. The fish that ate Osiris's member has been variously identified as *Lepidotus*, the Nile carp, *Phagrus* and *Oxyrynchus*, all of which were taboo in certain areas and at certain times. Isis manufactured a replacement phallus and attached it to Osiris's reassembled body (the first mummy) and successfully brought about his resurrection. Then, Isis turned herself into a Black Kite (the bird *Milvus migrans*) and mated with her husband. Isis and Nepthys are commonly depicted as Black Kites in funerary contexts, shown as mourners and protectors of the dead. Perhaps the plaintive screeches of these birds recalled the cries of mourning women to the ancient Egyptians, hence the birds' identification with these goddesses.

As a result of this union, Isis became pregnant, and retired to the town of Khemmis in the Delta where she gave birth to her son, Horus. Horus grew up in this protected area, nursed by his mother Isis and the goddess Hathor. When he came of age he emerged from the Delta and engaged in a series of dramatic battles with his uncle, Seth. This myth cycle is recounted in "The Contendings of Horus and Seth", which, according to some sources, took eighty years.

Ultimately Horus emerged victorious and was crowned king of Egypt, while Osiris, his father, became ruler of the dead and the Underworld. Seth was given control of the deserts and rainstorms and was associated with chaos and disorder, while Horus and Osiris were associated with *maat*. The living pharaoh is always identified with Horus and the deceased king with Osiris. Some scholars believe that the version of the myth preserved in the temple at Edfu might conceivably have had its roots in historical reality, being a record of a part of the civil war that convulsed Egypt in the late Second Dynasty. Other scholars suggest an earlier military engagement that took place between two rival rulers in the Predynastic period.

Other scholars have suggested that Osiris was one of the earliest gods of Egypt, who started out as a chthonic fertility god associated with the inundation and the growth of crops (hence his association with black and green as symbolic of rebirth and resurrection, and the annual Nile flood's association with rebirth), and later connected with the underworld. As the cult of Osiris spread, he took on the attributes of other gods whose cult centres he appropriated. In the myth cycle these other cult centres that are found throughout Egypt are explained by the distribution of the different body parts of Osiris, and thus the land of Egypt is a reflection of the body of Osiris.

Osiris's most famous cult centre, and the focus of many funerary beliefs and rituals, is Abydos in Middle Egypt. Osiris's head was deposited here by Seth after the dismemberment. By the Middle Kingdom the tomb of a First Dynasty ruler, King Djer, became identified as the tomb of Osiris, and the site became a major centre of pilgrimage. It is also in the Middle Kingdom that it became common for any dead person to take on the epithet, "Osiris N(ame of deceased)". Prior to that, this term was only associated with royalty. The Egyptians also believed that one access to the realm of the dead might be through a break in the cliffs at Abydos, which further intensified the religious significance of the site. Because of these associations, Abydos became a major cult centre and a focus for pilgrimage associated with regeneration. Many people chose to be buried at Abydos, while others erected memorial stelae at the site instead. The "pilgrimage to Abydos" was such an important part of funerary belief that it was featured in tombs in two-dimensional representations on the walls, as well as being represented by three-dimensional wooden boat models that showed the bier being taken to Abydos, thereby further ensuring the rebirth of the deceased.

Funerary deities

Osiris was, of course, the archetypal funerary deity. He was the ruler of the Underworld and the prototype mummy. He was responsible for judging the dead person and for deciding whether or not he was worthy of eternal life. His own resurrection through Isis's magic provides the foundation for the ancient Egyptian concept of life continuing after death, albeit in a transformed state. There were, however, other gods that were associated with the Afterlife.

The god responsible for mummification and for leading the deceased to the Underworld to be judged by Osiris was Anubis. In his role as guide between this world and the next he became associated with Charon in the Graeco-Roman period, and St Christopher in the early Christian period. Anubis is shown as a jackal-like creature or as a man with a jackal's head. It is probable that Anubis is represented as a super-canid, combining the most salient attributes of several types of canids, rather than being just a jackal or a dog. The connection with the jackal was probably due to a desire to protect the corpse from being dismembered by such animals that were known to prey off carrion and to frequent graveyards. By invoking such an animal, using sympathetic magic, the Egyptians presumably believed that Anubis would protect the corpse from any such harm. Thus he was also regarded as the guardian of the necropolis, a role that is reflected in one of his most common epithets: "lord of the sacred land" (*neb-ta-djeser*). Anubis was associated with mummification as he was supposed to have been responsible for wrapping Osiris; thus, many priests associated with the practice of mummification were identified with Anubis. In fact, during the course of the mummification and wrapping ritual, a priest would take on the persona of Anubis and wear an Anubis mask. A ceramic example of such a mask is now located in the Hildesheim Museum, and another possible cartonnage example is in the Egyptian Museum, Cairo. Anubis was also associated with Khentimentiu, another canine deity from Abydos, who was superseded by Osiris and whose identity was also syncretized with that of Anubis, as can be seen

by the title shared by all three gods: "Foremost Among the Westerners".

Osiris's wife and sister Isis, and Nepthys, his other sister, were also potent funerary deities. Both goddesses play an important role in protecting the mummy and bringing it safely to resurrection, hence the use of their images at the head and foot of coffins and sarcophagi. They are also frequently shown mourning the deceased, thus underlining the deceased's association with Osiris and the potential of rebirth. They are depicted as Black Kites or as women. Isis's insignia is a throne, while Nepthys's is a composite hieroglyphic symbol consisting of a basket and a building, which translates as her name and title, "Lady of the Mansion". These insignia are worn on the head.

Two other goddesses, Neith and Selqet, regularly join Isis and Nepthys in their protective roles. Neith was also known as a creator and a war goddess, whose insignia consists of a shield pierced by two arrows. Selqet is identified as a woman with a rearing scorpion on her head, and her name appears to be an abbreviation of a phrase that is translated as "the one who caused the throat to breathe". Presumably this title reflects her power over the sting of a scorpion, but it is also relevant to rebirth as she could cause the mummy to breathe again. In the Pyramid Texts (see below) she is associated with the embalming process.

Together, the four goddesses protect the coffin and the canopic chest, which contained the embalmed viscera of the deceased (see Chapters 3 and 5). Each of the four internal organs is also linked to a different demi-god, each one responsible for a separate organ. These gods are known collectively as the "Four Sons of Horus". Originally all were shown with human heads. However, from the Middle to the New Kingdom the divinities are personalized. Imseti is shown as a man and was responsible for protecting the liver; he was associated with Isis. Hapy had the head of a baboon and was in charge of the lungs; he was associated with Nepthys. Duamutef was canid headed and protected the stomach; he was

Anubis leading the deceased to the Netherworld. Valley of the Queens 44.

associated with Neith. Qebehsenuef was hawk headed and cared for the intestines; he was associated with Selqet. These protective demi-gods appear on canopic jars, on coffins, sarcophagi and other funerary equipment.

There are a myriad of other divine beings that are associated with the passage of the dead between their two lives, the judgement of the dead and their successful rebirth, and they are too numerous to mention. A few of the more significant ones are as follows. *Maat*, personified as a feather or a woman crowned with a feather, is featured in the judgement scene (see below). Thoth, the god of writing and recording who is often depicted as an ibis-headed man, took notes on the life of the deceased. Ammit, the Devourer of the Dead, was responsible for devouring the hearts of any evil dead whose hearts were heavier than the feather of *maat* and who were condemned to annihilation. Ammit is depicted as having a crocodile head, the foreparts of a lion and the rear of a hippopotamus.

Funerary books

Several funerary books that provide protection for the dead have been preserved from ancient Egypt. These are essentially guide-books or crib-notes that helped the deceased to enter the Afterlife safely. They supply spells that negate the threats and overcome the obstacles that riddled the route to the Afterlife.

The earliest such texts were exclusively for the use of royalty and were first found inscribed in the burial chamber of the pyramid of Unas (*c.* 2350 BC), the last king of the Fifth Dynasty. This has led to them being named Pyramid Texts. These texts appear in the pyramids of kings and queens of the Old Kingdom and comprise a total of some 800 spells or "utterances". Pyramid Texts are carved in vertical columns in sunk relief. They are frequently painted green or blue–green, alluding to the Osirian colour of rebirth, as well as to the sky to which the king ascends when he enters the eternal divine realm and becomes identified with

A papyrus showing the Judgement scene. The heart of the deceased is weighed against the feather of maat, with Thoth taking notes as to the outcome. Ammit sits ready to eat the deceased should his heart be too heavy. Cairo Museum.

Osiris. The spells are to aid the king in his ascent to the sky and to his reception into the kingdom of the gods. There are three main types of utterances: protective spells that keep the king safe from scorpions, snakes and other dangerous creatures; spells for the deceased to use in the Afterworld when using boats, ladders, etc. to travel safely; and the last set of incantations which is associated with the execution of funerary rituals, such as the Opening of the Mouth, a ritual that reanimates the mummy and restores its senses.

Although the Pyramid Texts were a perquisite of royalty in the Old Kingdom, they were usurped in their original format by non-royals extensively in the Late Period, as well as by a few officials of the Middle and New Kingdoms, who used only a selection of these texts on their sarcophagi.

Coffin Texts are a development of the Pyramid Texts, and take their name from the fact that they are inscribed inside non-royal coffins of the First Intermediate Period and the Middle Kingdom. They are a manifestation of one of the many usurpations of royal privileges that came about as a result of the turmoil of the First Intermediate Period. They offer a guarantee of an Afterlife

Pyramid Texts, filled with blue–green colour, from the pyramid of Pepi I. Saqqara.

associated with Osiris for *everyone* or, at least, everyone who could afford it. During this time it is not certain what funerary texts were used by royalty; certainly they would have been different from these, just as in the New Kingdom royal funerary texts were generally not employed by non-royal personages, albeit with exceptions. Despite their name, Coffin Texts are not restricted to coffins; they are found on mummy masks, tomb walls and sometimes even on papyri. Some of these texts are identical to those found in the Pyramid Texts, and their purpose is the same: to see the deceased safely through the tests and obstacles that mark the path to the Afterlife.

The Coffin Texts comprise at least 1185 spells and are generally written in hieratic, a cursive form of hieroglyphs. Unlike the Pyramid Texts, which are unillustrated, the Coffin Texts are occasionally enhanced with vignettes. Many of these vignettes appear in a compilation of spells, all of which are very different from those that appear in the Pyramid Texts. These spells are

These wooden images of Ptah-Sokar-Osiris were sometimes hollowed out in the back so that a funerary papyrus roll could be fitted into the aperture. Berlin.

maps and guides to the Hereafter and are illustrated by maps that show the way, with the correct passwords, to the Afterlife. The most famous book that stands out within these collective texts is The Book of Two Ways, with maps of the area appearing on the floor of the coffin's trough.

Coffin Texts included certain novelties when compared with Pyramid Texts, such as the desire to be reunified with loved ones in the Afterlife, as well as the battle with Apophis, a giant serpent who was the sworn enemy of the sun god, Re. The sun was a symbol of rebirth and resurrection as it rose in the east, traversed the sky and set in the west, repeating this cycle daily. To the

The sun god, Re, travelling on his barque with a benu bird at the prow. This sacred bird is associated with the cult of the sun god; its name derives from the Egyptian word meaning to rise (weben), and was a prototype of the phoenix. Photograph by J. Swanson.

Egyptians, the rising of the sun was its birth, its setting death and its rising the following day rebirth. Thus, the sun was one of the most significant symbols of resurrection in ancient Egypt. The deceased king would become one with the sun god and traverse the skies in his barque. From the Middle Kingdom on, any deceased person was identified with the sun god and followed the same trajectory. It is because of the sun's path that the West (*imenti*) was regarded as the appropriate place for burial and was another name for the land of the dead.

An interesting feature of both Pyramid and Coffin Texts is the mutilation of some of the hieroglyphs. The Egyptians believed that images, and by extension words comprising images, magically came alive and were powerful in themselves. To ensure that none of the hieroglyphs depicting dangerous animals came alive and disturbed the rest of the deceased, they were deliberately mutilated. Snakes are shown cut in half, birds are deprived of legs or beaks, and lions are only partially depicted. In the late Middle Kingdom and the Second Intermediate Period, scribes went to great lengths to substitute inanimate signs for animate ones wherever possible.

The Book of the Dead, perhaps the most famous of all Egyptian funerary texts, is first found in the early Seventeenth Dynasty in the coffin of Queen Mentuhotep and continued to be employed through the Late Period. It was probably compiled in the Theban area. The book, or more correctly "Coming Forth by Day", consists of about 200 spells or chapters. Many of these are derived from its predecessors, the Pyramid and Coffin Texts (both of which seem to have a Memphite origin), with the addition of new utterances. These spells were inscribed (generally in hieratic) on papyri, mummy cloths, amulets (especially Spells 30, 30B, 26, 27 and 29B on heart scarabs), shabtis (Spell 6; see Chapter 5 for more information), coffins and sometimes tomb walls. The Book of the Dead is lavishly embellished with vignettes that clarify and illustrate the utterances or chapters to which they allude.

As with the earlier funerary texts, the Book of the Dead served to provision, protect and guide the deceased to the Afterworld, which was largely located in the Fields of Reeds, an idealized Egypt. However, there are certain differences between it and its predecessors. There is a decline in the emphasis on a reunion with one's family, and there is an emphasis on the judgement of the dead so that the deceased could be regenerated. Chapter 125 was an innovation, and perhaps one of the most important spells to be added as it seems to reflect a change in morality. This chapter, accompanied by a vignette, shows the deceased before Osiris and forty-two judges, each representing a different aspect of *maat*. A part of the ritual was to name each judge correctly and give a "negative confession". The "negative confessions" consist of the deceased saying he had *not* lied, borne false witness, cheated, robbed, caused pain, killed, been rapacious, etc. The heart of the deceased is then weighed on a scale against the feather of *maat*: if it is unbalanced, it is given to Ammit; if it is balanced, then the deceased is allowed to proceed to the Afterlife.

The Book of the Dead, together with portions of the Pyramid and Coffin Texts, continued in use through the Roman Period, with more books being added to the corpus of funerary texts that were used for non-royal individuals. Later funerary texts that appear at the end of the Late Period and the Graeco-Roman period include two versions of the Books of Breathing. These come from Thebes, although the books themselves mention a divine origin relating to Isis, Osiris and Thoth. These books are roughly divided into fifteen sections and emphasize the survival of the deceased's name in the Afterlife, the avoidance of a second death (end of breathing) and a continuation of life. Another composition, the Book of Traversing Eternity, is similar in its intention. In addition to being written on papyri, these texts were sometimes inscribed on wooden boards that were laid beneath the mummy.

There are several other funerary texts that date from the New Kingdom onward, termed the Books of the Underworld. Royal burials (and a few private burial chambers that aped them) contained separate texts that detailed the voyage of the sun god through the netherworld during the twelve hours of the night until his successful rebirth in the morning. The geography of the Hereafter is thus also described in these books. These books are standard and unchanging, in contrast to the Coffin Texts and the Book of the Dead that have different versions, some with more and others with fewer spells. The illustrations found in the Books of the Underworld are integrated into the text and not separate vignettes as those in the Book of the Dead. Throughout the New Kingdom these texts were predominantly reserved for royalty, although there are a few examples of non-royal individuals using them. It is only after the end of the New Kingdom that they became more commonly usurped by non-royal individuals. Interestingly, during the Third Intermediate Period, the Book of the Dead became used extensively in royal tombs, reversing the previous emphasis.

The most important of these funerary texts are the Book of the Amduat, or the Book of What is in the Underworld, and the Book of Gates (named for the large gates that guard each hour). These two texts are organized according to the twelve hours of the night, with the ram-headed nocturnal form of the sun god located in the centre of each hour. The sun god illuminates each nocturnal hour, bringing life and resurrecting the dead to be judged. These books differ from other Books of the Underworld where the barque of the sun god is almost entirely absent, although the presence of the god is indicated by a red sun disc. These books are frequently oriented in the tomb so that they start in the west and end in the east, thus imitating the path of the sun god's barque on its route to rebirth. Later books, such as the Book of Caverns, replace the division of the night into twelve hours by a division into six sectors. However, all these books share the idea that the deceased is identified with the sun god, and like him must be safely steered through the perils of the night hours to ensure his safe rebirth, and that of the cosmos, on the following day.

After the Amarna period a new group of Books of the Afterlife developed: the Books of the Sky. Although the sun still plays an important role, the focus has changed somewhat. The sky goddess, Nut, is shown, thus indicating a celestial Afterlife. The sun is shown traversing the sky, or the body of Nut, and being swallowed by her in the evening, to be born the next day. Although the setting for the Afterlife has changed to a celestial one, the path and the travails encountered are similar to those found in the Netherworld. The Book of Nut, the Book of the Night and the Book of the Day are some of these celestial books. The last of these is unusual in that it describes the diurnal rather than nocturnal voyage of the sun god.

Other funerary books that are primarily royal are the Litany of Re and the Book of the Heavenly Cow. These texts differ from their predecessors in the absence of illustrations, despite having a similar content. The Litany of Re focuses on the role of Re as the source of rebirth, caretaker and protector of the blessed, and punisher of the wrong-doer. The Book of the Heavenly Cow appears in royal tombs and is unlike other funerary books as it concerns the large-scale salvation of mankind, rather than the regeneration and rebirth of a specific individual.

3
Mummification

A mummy is the artificially preserved body of a human or an animal and is the quintessential manifestation of death in ancient Egypt. Mummies were produced in ancient Egypt from perhaps as early as the late Naqada II period until the Christian era, in an effort to preserve the earthly body for the use of the *ka* and the *ba*. The Egyptian word for mummy is *sah*; the modern word, mummy, is derived from the Persian and Arabic words for wax and bitumen, *muum* and *mumia*, thence mummy. The Arabs who first came upon mummies mistakenly thought that they had achieved their dark colour by being covered with bitumen. Bitumen is a black pitch-like substance occurring naturally in Persia and in the area of the Dead and Red Seas, which was sporadically used in the mummification process of some individuals from the late New Kingdom onward.

The history of mummies

Although the Egyptians created mummies to be sealed in their tombs for eternity, the vicissitudes of fate have often intervened. Tombs and mummies have always been the focus of tomb-robbers, some of whom entered tombs shortly after the burial or even formed part of the burial party. Indeed, there are cases in which mummies were despoiled while still in the hands of the embalmers. Records on papyrus, dating from the Twentieth Dynasty, feature trials of various tomb-robbers who had violated royal tombs. The most significant of these documents are the Ambras, Leopold II-Amherst, Harris A and Mayer A and B Papyri. The punishment for such desecration was death and, for the plundering of royal tombs, death by impalement and the obliteration of the wrong-doer's name, thus condemning him to oblivion for all eternity. This tradition of tomb robbing, with less dire punishments, continued into the modern period as tomb-robbers plundered graves and destroyed mummies in search of amulets, grave-goods or the mummies themselves so that they could be sold to tourists as souvenirs or to less scrupulous museums as exhibits (see Chapter 7).

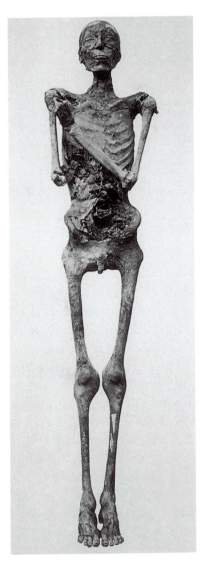

The mummy of Seti II with his arms crossed over his chest. His embalming incision was quite large and left a gaping hole. Cairo Museum.

It was not only greed and curiosity that contributed to the destruction of mummies but the mistaken idea that they, and especially the bitumen that covered them, were a crucial ingredient in medicine. Abd el-Latif, a twelfth-century Arab scientist, recorded how *mum* from the mummy mountain in Persia mixes with water and produces an odour that cures diseases when it is inhaled or, better yet, when the mixture is ingested. This idea maintained its popularity: even as recently as in the nineteenth century the King of Persia sent Queen Victoria small amounts of *mum* for her health. From AD 50, mummies were mentioned in lists of materia medica and continued to be used in both oriental and occidental prescriptions. After the twelfth century AD, the use of mummies in medicine became commonplace in the occident, and the word "mumie" or "mumia" appeared frequently in Latin medical texts. Mummy was used for all kinds of ailments including abscesses, eruptions, fractures, concussions, paralysis, hemicrania, epilepsy, vertigo, spitting of blood from the lungs, throats, coughs, nausea, ulcers, poisons and disorders of the liver and spleen. Mummies as medicine were so common that they are even mentioned in literary texts: Shakespeare's apothecary in *Romeo and Juliet* stocks mummy. As one might expect, such widespread use resulted in an active trade in mummies and contributed to their destruction and that of the tombs whence they came.

Tourists bought mummies, or even portions of mummies, as curiosities, a custom that later led to the unwrapping of mummies for show. For the most part this was unscientific work, resulting in the destruction of many mummies, although it did lead to later unwrappings where mummies and their bandaging techniques were carefully studied. Such analyses formed the basis of some of our knowledge of the science of mummification.

The origins of mummification

Traditionally Egyptologists have thought that the idea for mummification arose after the Predynastic period when the bodies of the dead were buried in simple, shallow, pit graves in the desert sand. The sand naturally desiccated the bodies, leaving them as relatively intact shells. These naturally preserved bodies might have been accidentally uncovered later on by animals, such as dogs or jackals, or by wind erosion, thus giving the Egyptians the idea of artificially preserving their dead so that the bodies could be used in the Afterlife. Until recently, it had been thought that mummification started during the Dynastic period.

However, the results of recent excavations at the sites of Hierakonpolis and Adaima in the south of Egypt have modified this view of the inception of mummification. At both these sites, graves from the Naqada II period have shown attempts at the artificial preservation of the body, with the use of resin and bandages. It is also possible that evisceration might have been practised on some of these bodies. These findings are forcing Egyptologists to re-evaluate their ideas about the origins of mummification, which seem to be much earlier than hitherto thought. The inspiration for the artificial preservation of the bodies might not lie in the practical examples of naturally desiccated corpses but, rather, in Egyptian religious thought.

A curious feature of some of the wrapped corpses found at Hierakonpolis and Adaima is that a few of these have heads deliberately separated from their bodies and placed on the chest, often clasped between the upraised hands. Cut-marks on the vertebrae of

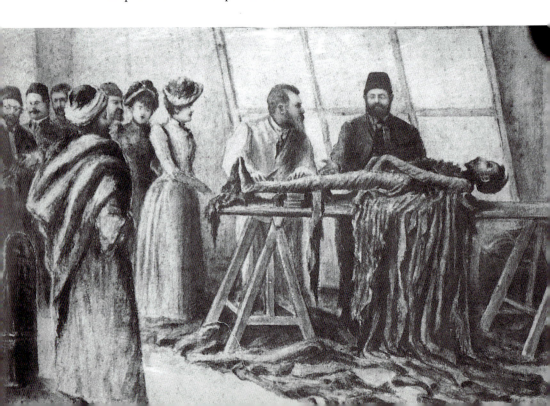

several mummies support the idea of a deliberately mutilated body, rather than a perfectly preserved intact body. It is possible that this practice had its roots in a religious ritual. The only religious texts that shed any light on this are the Pyramid Texts and Coffin Texts. Utterance 373 of the Pyramid Texts recounts how the dismembered body of the king, a parallel to the dismembered corpse of Osiris, is reconstituted for resurrection, with the reattachment of the head being a primary part of the regenerative process:

Oho! Oho! Arise, O King!
Take your head,
Gather your bones,
Gather your limbs ...
... Rise up, O King, for you shall not perish!

Such religious texts, in addition to the finds from the two sites, have rekindled an Egyptological debate: were the earliest mummies defleshed? Defleshing entails removing all the flesh from the bones prior to bandaging. Early excavators, notably W. M. F. Petrie and H. Junker, claimed to have excavated corpses that had been defleshed from the sites of Giza, Meidum and Deshasheh, as well as from some Predynastic cemeteries. In both the Giza and the Meidum cemeteries several bodies showed that the bandages were in direct contact with the bone and in some cases the skeletons were not properly articulated. The absence of flesh is not ominous: natural decomposition of tissue, often due to improper or poor quality mummification, causes the flesh to crumble and the bandages to slip down, close to the bone. However, the disarticulation of skeletons in addition to the absence of flesh fuelled the excavators' idea of ritual defleshing; in fact, Petrie even went so far as to suggest that the flesh might have been ritually consumed, alluding to references made in the Pyramid and Coffin Texts. Some of the disarticulated corpses found at Adaima might support this idea for the Predynastic period. However, the evidence for this practice is unsubstantiated for the pharaonic period. Further investigations might clarify this issue and provide alternative suggestions about the origins of mummification.

Unwrapping mummies was fashionable both in Egypt and abroad. These unwrappings became very social events, with food and drink following the unwrapping. Egyptian Museum.

Sources of information

Information concerning mummification is derived from numerous sources, although none of these includes any sort of instruc-
tion manual written by the ancient Egyptians. The Egyptians are
curiously silent about modes of mummification, in both their
written and their figurative sources, although a rare representation of a portion of the procedure is shown on the Late Period
coffin of Djedbastiuefankh, now in the Pelzaeus Museum in
Hildesheim. The Rhind Magical Papyrus (c. 200 BC) provides
some information on rituals associated with it, and three papyri
in the Cairo, Durham Oriental and Louvre Museums, all dating
to approximately the first century AD, provide some spells to be
recited while bandaging up each part of the body. Another
papyrus, in Berlin, also gives some instructions about the order in
which limbs were to be wrapped, amulets inserted and spells
recited. Some of the earliest writings on mummies come from the
fifth century BC Ionian Greek writer, Herodotus, closely followed and augmented by the account of Diodorus Siculus in the
first century BC, and rounded out by the writings of Porphyry in
the third century AD. In addition to the few Egyptian texts and
Classical sources, information concerning mummification can be
derived from examinations of mummies, embalming caches,
modern scientific tests and experimental work.

The scientific examination of mummies, and the testing of their
tissues, also contributes information about how mummification
took place. The identification of many of the substances used in
mummification, such as different desiccants and resins, has been
confirmed, as has some of the methodology. Experimental work
on humans, carried out by Bob Brier and Ronn Wade, or animals, carried out by the Manchester Mummy Project in the
1970s, and by Salima Ikram more recently in the 1990s, has
also contributed to a better understanding of the actual process
of mummification. Embalming caches, where all the waste
material from embalming was carefully buried, also provide
practical information about mummification as they contain

residues of the materials used in the process, as well as some of the tools required.

The process and materials of mummification

The goal of mummification was to desiccate and preserve the body. Book II of Herodotus's *Histories* provides a detailed account of the procedure as it was performed in his time. Coupled with the records of Diodorus, this has long provided the basis for the study of the techniques of mummification. Herodotus's description of mummification, although relatively late in date, describes three types of embalming, one for every economic group:

> When a body is brought to the embalmers, they produce specimen models in wood, graded in quality ... They ask which of the three is required, and the family of the dead, having agreed upon a price, leave the embalmers to their task.

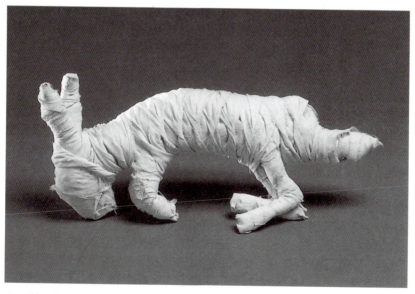

A rabbit that was successfully mummified using a turpentine enema. American University in Cairo, photograph by F. Dzikowski.

The most perfect process is as follows: as much as possible of the brain is removed via the nostrils with an iron hook, and what cannot be reached with the hook is washed out with drugs; next, the flank is opened with a flint knife and the whole contents of the abdomen removed; the cavity is then thoroughly cleaned and washed out, firstly with palm wine and again with an infusion of ground spices. After that, it is filled with pure myrrh, cassia, and every other aromatic substance, excepting frankincense, and sewn up again, after which the body is placed in natron [see below], covered entirely over, for seventy days – never longer. When this period is over, the body is washed and then wrapped from head to foot in linen cut into strips and smeared on the underside with gum, which is commonly used by the Egyptians instead of glue. In this condition the body is given back to the family, who have a wooden case made, shaped like a human figure, into which it is put.

When, for reasons of expense, the second quality is called for, the treatment is different: no incision is made and the intestines are not removed, but oil of cedar is injected with a syringe into the body through the anus which is afterwards stopped up to prevent the liquid from escaping. The body is then cured in natron for the prescribed number of days, on the last of which the oil is drained off. The effect of it is so powerful that as it leaves the body it brings with it the viscera in a liquid state, and as the flesh has been dissolved by the natron, nothing of the body is left but the skin and bones. After this treatment, it is returned to the family without further attention.

The third method, used for embalming the bodies of the poor, is simply to wash out the intestines, and keep the body for seventy days in natron.[1]

The key ingredient in the mummification was natron, or *netjry*, divine salt. It is a mixture of sodium bicarbonate, sodium carbonate, sodium sulphate and sodium chloride that occurs naturally in Egypt, most commonly in the Wadi Natrun some sixty-four kilometres northwest of Cairo. It has desiccating and defatting properties and was the preferred desiccant, although common salt was also used in more economical burials, especially in the Christian period. Corpses were placed on embalming tables or beds on a pile of natron, their openings filled with small bags of the substance, and more of the same material piled on top of them. The natron had to be changed regularly, as once it absorbed the bodily fluids it ceased being effective until it had dried. Embalming beds or tables were slanted wooden boards with raised cross-pieces that allowed the fluids to drain.

Other materials used in mummification, such as myrrh, other resins and spices, and oils, were used throughout the history of mummification. Resins, the sap secreted from fir and pine trees, especially, were imported into Egypt from Lebanon and Syria (cedar, fir and pine resin) and from Southern Arabia and East Africa (frankincense and myrrh). Resins were used, in a melted state, to fill the cranium and body cavity and to coat coffins, as they inhibit bacteria and deodorize. Oils of various sorts, including imported oils such as juniper and cedar, as well as domestic products such as lettuce and castor oils, were used to scent the corpse as well as to return flexibility to the desiccated limbs prior to wrapping.

Many of the materials used for mummification have been recovered from embalming caches. These caches, found all over Egypt in cemeteries, contain the detritus of mummification. As anything associated with this activity was deemed sacred, it could not be disposed of as ordinary rubbish, and thus had to be buried in a sacred area, i.e. in the necropolis. An embalming cache from Tutankhamun's interment was recovered in the early part of the nineteenth century.

Herodotus's three methods of mummification can be seen illustrated on various Egyptian funerary objects. These methods of mummification were common during the time that he was writing, the fifth century BC. However, one should bear in mind that mummification did not remain static throughout Egyptian history and evolved through time. Furthermore, one should also remember that more than one type of mummification technology could be employed at any one time. This might be determined by the preferred style of any one group of embalmers or the economic level of the deceased.

Classic (Eighteenth Dynasty) mummification is very similar to Herodotus's first method. It involves removing the brain through the left nostril. This was achieved by inserting a metal tool into the nostril and breaking through the ethmoid bone. A sharp metal tool would then slash and chop at the brain, thus liquefying it for its convenient removal through the nostril using a hooked implement. Melted resin would then be introduced through the nostril which would be stopped with a linen plug. The viscera were then removed by a cut in the left flank. These would be washed and treated separately, after which they were wrapped and placed in canopic jars (Chapter 5). The body cavity was washed with water and wine, and then the body was immersed, inside and out, in dry natron. After the requisite amount of time had passed, the body would be removed from the natron, oiled to return some flexibility to the limbs and then wrapped in bandages and prepared for burial.

Wrapping the corpse was a very important part of the mummification process. The bandages provided not only a physical barrier and protection for the body but a magico-religious one as well. As the mummy bandages, *wyt* or *wenkhyt* in Egyptian, were wound around the mummified corpse, special spells would be read out by a lector priest. These spells, reified by the bandages, would serve to enclose and protect the deceased. Thus, the cloth cocoon of a completely wrapped mummy, interspersed with amulets (see Chapter 5), would provide both physical and metaphysical protection for the mummy and contribute to the deceased's safe arrival in the Hereafter.

The length of time that mummification took seems to have been fairly standard throughout Egyptian history. Egyptian sources agree with Herodotus that mummification took a total of seventy days, with approximately forty days being used for the drying, and the remainder for wrapping and entombment. In the Theban tomb of Djehuty (TT 110) a text reads "A goodly burial arrives in peace, thy seventy days have been fulfilled in thy place of embalming". However, there are exceptions to this: an inscription from the tomb of Queen Meresankh III at Giza records that she was buried 272 days after her death – 202 days beyond the standard seventy days. Another individual, Pashenptah, a High Priest of Memphis in the Ptolemaic Period, also had an embalmment that lasted for 200 days, again for unknown reasons. This standard seventy-day period for embalmment might have been derived from the seventy-day disappearance and reappearance cycle of the star Sirius. Sirius was associated with Osiris, god of the Afterworld, who, like the star, vanished for seventy days before being resurrected.

The who and where of embalming

Embalming priests were associated with Anubis, and some even wore masks, taking on the persona of the god as part of the mummification ritual. The priests would all have had some knowledge of anatomy and mummification procedures. Ancient Egyptian texts are once more silent on the subject, although the classical sources are more forthcoming. Herodotus records that the embalmers were a special set of men belonging to different workshops, who had, as with any trade, a hereditary calling. Third century BC documents describe different embalmers' guilds, and the amounts they charged for materials and services. According to Diodorus Siculus the embalmers were respected as they were responsible for one's eternal preparation and last viewing on earth. However, not all members of this guild were well treated. Diodorus mentions one unfortunate member of the embalmers' group, the "slitter", the man responsible for making the flank incision for removing the viscera. According to Diodorus, the slitter flees immediately after making the incision, chased by the other embalmers and passers-by, who all hurl stones and abuse at him for violating a corpse.

Embalming, from the initial stages of washing the body to the desiccation of the corpse, took place in or near the necropolis in a series of workshops and temporary shelters. The *per ankh* (house of life) was the building which probably contained the written knowledge concerning mummification and the religious rituals surrounding it. Embalming started with washing the corpse. This was done at a structure termed the *ibw en wab* (tent of purification) or the *seh-netjer* (divine booth). In the Old Kingdom the former term was used for non-royals and the latter for royalty, although the latter term became commonly used for both groups in later periods. This was a temporary tent-like structure where the body was initially washed; it was conveniently located near a body of water, either the river or a canal. Excavators have uncovered some temporary buildings made of mud brick located at the entrance to certain tombs, which they have tentatively identified

as embalming workshops, *wabt net wet*, for the nobles buried there. Such structures have been found in front of the tombs of Nefer and Kai at Giza.

Development of mummification

Predynastic

Until the recent work at Hierakonpolis and Adaima, it was generally believed that burials of the Predynastic period were relatively simple, consisting only of naturally desiccated individuals placed in shallow graves cut into the desert gravel, together with a few grave goods. However, the recent excavations at the above-mentioned sites show that by the Naqada II period an active attempt was being made to protect and preserve the bodies of the deceased by wrapping them in linen, using linen padding to protect fragile portions of the anatomy, and employing resins to deodorize and preserve. Further excavations at these and other sites will no doubt change our knowledge about the history of mummification in this early period.

Archaic and Old Kingdom

Very few mummies survive from the Early Dynastic period. The ones that survive have been found wrapped in linen and placed in a flexed position in rectangular clay or wood coffins, with their arms at the sides. Some bodies, dating to the First Dynasty from Tarkhan, were placed on beds, a practice that was revived in the Graeco-Roman period in Egypt and in the Meroitic period in Nubia. In all of the Tarkhan burials the viscera were left intact. It is possible that the bandages were treated with natron and liquid resin, but unfortunately none of the bodies found from the First Dynasty were scientifically tested. The earliest royal mummy-part found is the bandaged and bejewelled arm of King Djer – or perhaps his wife, as a female skull was also found in the tomb – which was recovered in 1900 by Petrie

The mummification process is completed by a priest dressed as Anubis, wearing a mask, while the mummy is laid out on a funerary bed shaped like a lion, a solar and protective symbol. Priestesses in the guise of Isis and Nephthys flank the bed and carry out funerary rituals. Cairo Museum.

Thuyu's golden embalming wound cover. The incision was pulled together and then sealed with wax. Later, especially in Dynasty XXI, the cut was sewn up with linen thread. Cairo Museum.

from the king's tomb at Abydos, but never examined. It was sent to the Cairo Museum, divested of the bracelets that adorned the wrist and then discarded by the curator, Emile Brugsch. Fortunately, the mummy of a woman from the Second Dynasty found in 1911 by James Quibell at Saqqara was more closely studied and provides more information about mummification in this early period. The body, probably desiccated with natron, lay flexed on its side. Its wrappings were interesting as each limb was separately wrapped, and the outermost layer was worked to indicate the genitalia. This sort of detailed modelling became the norm in the Old Kingdom, and on these stylistic grounds it is possible that the elaborately bandaged and modelled foot found in the Step Pyramid's burial chamber might indeed belong to King Djoser, although some of the carbon-14 dates do not support this theory. In the Old Kingdom a definite effort was made to create an image of the deceased, using the wrappings. Two famous Fifth Dynasty examples of similarly well-modelled bodies are the mummies from the tomb of Nefer at Saqqara. Other mummies from Giza also had an extensive plaster coating applied to the linen, creating a carapace which was also well modelled and painted. This treatment transformed the body into an image of itself.

This method of mummification continued to be used throughout the Old Kingdom with a few innovations being made in succeeding dynasties. Evisceration was introduced by the Fourth Dynasty. The earliest surviving visceral container (see Chapter 5) comes from the Fourth Dynasty burial of Queen Hetepheres, the mother of King Khufu. Although the queen's mummy was not found, her canopic chest, containing visceral packages in a weak solution of natron in water, was recovered. The removal of the internal organs rendered the body less susceptible to putrefaction. The viscera were removed from a vertical incision in the left side of the body, with the resulting cavities filled with linen after desiccation was completed.

The First Intermediate Period and Middle Kingdom

As with the Early Dynastic period, there is little evidence of mummified remains that survive from the First Intermediate Period. The examples that exist are prepared in a way similar to that used in the Old Kingdom. The bodies are cured in dry natron, eviscerated and bandaged, with the viscera being separatedly dried and placed in canopic chests. The practice of moulding the wrappings declined by the end of the Old Kingdom, being replaced by simpler bandaging that spiralled around the body. An exception to this is the unusual Eleventh Dynasty mummy of Djehutynakht from Deir el-Bersha. His head is treated in a manner similar to that of Old Kingdom mummies, with the face covered by modelled linen, with the facial features detailed in paint. This head is remarkable in that its brain was removed through the nose, a development that sporadically featured in Middle Kingdom mummies. The facial modelling common in the Old Kingdom was replaced by cartonnage masks that covered the face and chest of the deceased (Chapter 5).

Methods of mummification diversified in the Middle Kingdom. The Old Kingdom method of evisceration through the left flank continued, but Herodotus's second method, using a cedar or juniper oil enema, was also introduced during this period. The majority of corpses that are thus treated are of Theban origin, coming from Deir el-Bahari, and belong to women related in some way to Mentuhotep II. The bodies of many of these individuals were so well preserved that elaborate tattoos are visible on the arms and abdomens of certain of the women.

The princesses whose corpses are prepared in this innovative manner were dried using natron, with a thin resin layer coating the skin. There were no evisceration cuts in the flank, although their torsos were, for the most part, devoid of internal organs. There were indications, however, that the viscera were dissolved and partially extracted through the rectum. Princesses Henhenet and Ashayet, and the burials in Deir el-Bahari (DBXI.24 and 26), all had dilated recta and vaginae, and some had bits of tissue, mainly intestines, projecting from the anus. Quite probably, an oleoresin, akin to turpentine, was injected into the anus in order to dissolve the organs, with partial success. Turpentine is made of resin and could easily have been produced and used for this purpose. Herodotus cites cedar oil being used for this purpose, although juniper oil is a more probable candidate as it is more effective and more strongly scented. Furthermore, it has been suggested that the bodies might have been filled with resin from the same orifice as some shiny particles were found adhering to Ashayet's rectum. Analysis of these particles, however, shows that this identification is doubtful. No excerebration was carried out on these mummies: all of the skulls contained brains. However, there is some debate as to whether the dilated recta and vaginae and tissue projections were due to a particular mummification technique or to other reasons. Some scholars disagree with the viability of the turpentine method and posit that the bodies had partially decayed prior to mummification and that the changes were due to the decay rather than the method of mummification. However, they cannot satisfactorily explain the absence of internal organs.

Experimental work on rabbits, carried out by Salima Ikram, has proven the efficacy of the turpentine method as a feasible method of mummification. A turpentine–juniper oil enema was administered to a dead rabbit, after which the anal aperture was plugged with a piece of linen. The rabbit was desiccated in natron for twenty-one days (the size of the animal meant that the traditional forty days were not required). Then the plug was removed and the turpentine, together with the now liquid internal organs (save for the heart which did not disintegrate), were squeezed out of the body. Then the rabbit was oiled, wrapped and prepared for burial in the same way that a conventionally preserved corpse would be. Three years later the rabbit that was mummified in this manner remains successfully preserved.

Other innovations of the Middle Kingdom include variations in arm positions: while some mummies kept their arms at the side, others, such as the Eleventh Dynasty mummy of Wah, had his arms folded over the chest. The removal of the brain occurs sporadically in mummies of this period; it did not become the norm until the New Kingdom. Bandaging during this period is protective. The limbs are bandaged spirally, many times over, and then the entire body is wrapped spirally, forming a cocoon. A shroud

The head of Sequenenre Tao showing the head wounds that were the cause of his death. Cairo Museum.

is finally placed over the body, and another over the face, which is further protected by a mask. Shrouds tended to be of plain linen, or fringed sheets, at this time.

An unusual example of swift and economical mummification due to extenuating circumstances comes from Tomb MMA 507, located near the tomb of Mentuhotep II in Thebes. This Middle Kingdom mass burial contained sixty corpses wrapped in layers of linen. These were clearly the bodies of soldiers who had fought and died in battle. The bodies of these soldiers had been scoured with sand and wrapped in linen without evisceration. Most of them had died violently in battle some distance from Thebes. This was attested by the arrow-tips protruding from the chest of one, the crushed skulls and knife marks of others. These veterans had lain exposed on the battlefield long enough to be attacked by birds of prey: signs of pecking and tearing of the flesh were evident. At the end of the battle these brave warriors were gathered up, hastily desiccated in sand and wrapped up and entombed near their homes in Thebes.

The Second Intermediate Period and the New Kingdom

Virtually no Hyksos mummies exist, so it is impossible to judge how their burial practices differed from those of the Egyptians. The few graves found are much damaged by water, and contain skeletons and grave goods. The majority of the information concerning the Second Intermediate Period comes from Thebes and provides the basis of knowledge concerning mummification during this period.

By this time excerebration was more common; several of the mummies found had empty crania. Arm positions become more standard: women's arms lie along their sides with the hands resting on their thighs, while men's arms are so arranged that their hands cover their genitalia. Care was taken in mummification: an elderly woman had hair extensions so that she could be more attractive throughout eternity. Hair extensions and even toupées have been found at Hierakonpolis as early as the Naqada II period.

The majority of New Kingdom mummies found date to the Eighteenth and early Nineteenth Dynasties and include both royal and non-royal examples. This large body of material not only provides information about changes in mummification but illustrates differences in mummification between classes. Royal mummies tended to be prepared with more expensive materials and their arm positions, crossed over the chest, are different from those of non-royal individuals who continued the arm placement common in the Second Intermediate Period. It should be remembered that, along with the innovations in mummification that were introduced during this period, older and more economical methods of preserving the body continued to be concurrently used. Interestingly, the royal tomb workmen from Deir el-Medina, although possessing finely decorated coffins, were only wrapped in linen, not treated with natron or resin, until the early

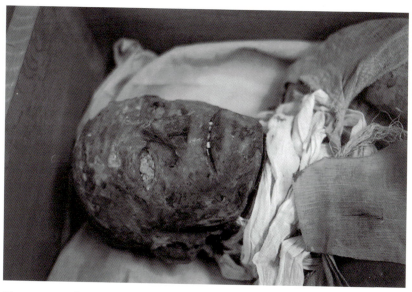

The mummy of Ramesses III had some of its facial features enhanced with paint. This mummy was unusual in being covered by a cut-out linen crocodile. Cairo Museum.

Nineteenth Dynasty. This suggests an extension of the technique in the years following the Amarna Period.

At this time excerebration by breaking through the ethmoid bone became standard. An exception to this method is King Ahmose, whose brain was removed by partially separating his head from his body, and removing the brain through the foramen magna. Resin was lavishly used during this period, as were oils. The wealthier the burial, the more these two ingredients were used. When over-used these materials do not help in the preservation of the corpse; rather, the reverse. Too much oil and resin eats away the flesh, and can eventually reduce a corpse to powder. The location of the incision also changed during this time: prior to the reign of Thutmose III it was vertical, thereafter it was diagonal, following the line of the iliac crest. During the course of the New Kingdom increasing efforts were made to render the body more lifelike, a practice that reached an acme in the Twenty-first Dynasty. Small pieces of linen with cursory eyes drawn upon them have been placed over the eye, providing new eyes for the mummies. In the Twentieth Dynasty, Ramesses IV had small onions inserted under his eyelids and used as eyes. From the Nineteenth Dynasty onwards, the body was stuffed very carefully with linen, sawdust or lichen, so as to better retain its natural shape. Ramesses II's dis-tinctive nose was packed with seeds and a small animal bone to make it withstand the pressure of the bandages applied during mummification. Special attention was paid to finger- and toe-nails by tying them on with string so that they would not separ-ate during desiccation, while early Eighteenth Dynasty royal genitalia were frequently tied to a thigh so they would not fall off during the drying process.

Mummies of this period are well wrapped in linen bandages of varying qualities. These bandages either were purchased from the embalmer's workshop or came from the deceased's household. The bandages were wound about the extremities and limbs spi-rally and around the torso. The entire body was then wrapped together with bandages and ultimately a shroud, which was kept

Nodjmet is an example of the overenthusiasm of the embalmers of Dynasty XXI: her face was so overstuffed, and the materials used were incompatible, that the skin of her cheek burst open. She has recently been conserved. Cairo Museum.

in place by vertical and horizontal bandages. Most shrouds were plain, although some painted examples, showing the deceased before an offering table, have been found at Deir el-Medina.

The Third Intermediate Period onward

Mummification technology reached its zenith in the Twenty-first Dynasty. During this time the embalmers started to turn the prepared body into a more perfect image of itself. Unlike in the Old Kingdom when bandages and plaster had been used to achieve this effect, in the Twenty-first Dynasty this was accomplished by manipulating the flesh. Several incisions were made in the body, described in the Rhind Magical Papyrus, and these were used to stuff the body with subcutaneous packing of mud, sand and sawdust, until the body took on the shape that it had enjoyed in life. There are even examples of old and sick people being restored to their former healthy forms, thanks to the embalmers' arts. An elderly lady who had been suffering from bedsores on her back had these repaired with gazelle skin. Some embalmers were too enthusiastic, and some mummies, or parts thereof, split open owing to a combination of over-packing and the chemical reactions of the packing materials. During this period bodies were not only stuffed but also painted: red for men and yellow for women. This imitates the colours used to designate each gender in Egyptian art. Facial features such as eyebrows, lips, etc. were cosmetically enhanced, and glass and stone eyes inserted into the eyesockets. The viscera, instead of being placed in canopic jars, were returned to the body in separately wrapped packets after desiccation and wrapped with the rest of the body. Although thus no longer being used for their primary purpose, the tradition and symbolism of canopic containers was such that they continued to accompany some interments. Indeed, certain tombs had solid dummies, while one king had dummy packages of viscera in his jars (see Chapter 5). The emphasis in the Twenty-first Dynasty was definitely to preserve the whole body as an intact and lifelike unit. Innovations were also made in wrapping the body. In addition to spirally bandaging the extremities and limbs, the torso was wrapped in a figure of eight that served to strengthen and support it. Then it was covered by a shroud that was sometimes embellished with an image of Osiris.

After the Twenty-first Dynasty the quality of mummification started to decline, with stuffing and painting being abandoned, although the body cavity was still filled. The brain continued to be removed via the nose until the Saite period. The major change in mummification was the placing of the four visceral packets on top of the thighs rather than within the body cavity, after a short revival of "real" canopic jars late in the Twenty-fifth Dynasty. From the Twenty-sixth to the Thirtieth Dynasty, the visceral packages were placed between the thighs or lower down, between the legs. Sometimes empty canopic jars were still placed in the burial chambers, although such objects disappear from the record at the start of the Ptolemaic period. Clearly these empty jars were kept in the tombs for their symbolic value rather than for any

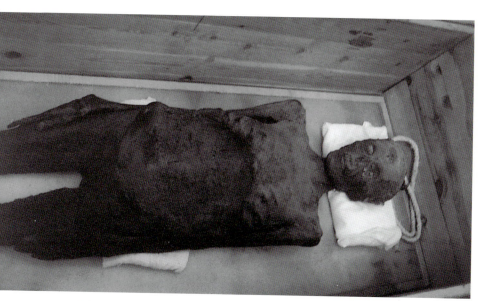

A female mummy from the Roman period. Her eyes are covered with gold foil, and she appears to have been mummified using turpentine. Cairo Museum.

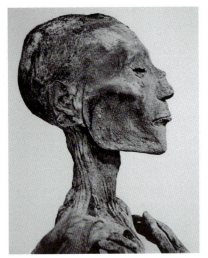

Ramesses V's face is marked with spots, presumably the remains of a bout of smallpox that he survived. Cairo Museum.

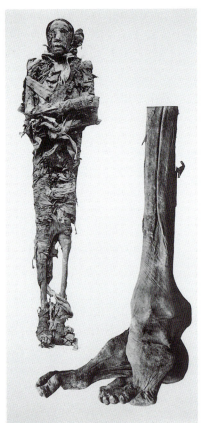

Siptah and his leg, a possible result of polio. Cairo Museum.

practical purpose (see Chapter 5). Some Late Period mummies show that efforts were made at eviscerating individuals from the anus, without the benefit of turpentine or other solvents. These attempts have left lacerations in the rectal area. In the Saite period the removal of the brain became less common, and there are instances of evisceration taking place through the right rather than the left side. Non-royal individuals also start to have their hands placed across the chest, although some of the earlier arm positions continue to be used for both men and women. Toward the end of the dynastic period the majority of mummies were shoddily prepared with little evisceration or excerebration being practised, with the latter being totally abandoned by the second century AD. Rather, the corpses were swiftly dried, covered with resin or sometimes bitumen, and hastily wrapped. Only a few examples of good quality mummification come from the later periods of Egyptian history.

In the Ptolemaic and early Roman Periods when the viscera were removed from the body they were often placed between the legs with empty canopic boxes occasionally also being present in the tomb. A few Roman period embalmers were as dedicated to their craft as their predecessors. Some mummies have been found that were damaged before death, or during mummification, and the embalmers have taken pains to restore the bodies so that they are whole for the Afterlife: detached heads are reattached with palm ribs, and substitutes are provided for missing limbs.

Although the quality of mummification varied considerably in the later periods of Egyptian history, the wrapping of mummies improved tremendously in the Graeco-Roman period. The body was carefully wrapped up in large numbers of horizontally wound bandages which were covered with elaborate polychrome shrouds decorated with images of Isis and Nepthys, texts, figures of the deceased or vignettes from one of the Underworld books surrounding a large mummy figure making up the centre of the composition. These decorations on the shrouds are of the same type as would have been found in tomb-chapels of the period.

The Roman period continues this model, as well as producing the most elaborate external bandages of all periods. From the first and second centuries AD, the outermost layer of bandages consists of distinctive rhomboid coffers. Often each coffer was held in place by a gold or gilded stud, or the bandages were wrapped over a small piece of gold foil, leaving it exposed at the bottom of the bandage-coffering. Sometimes multi-coloured bandages were used so as to vary the colour of each. This rhomboid patterning was popularly used with mummies that had wooden portrait panels wrapped into the bandages, occurring between the first and third centuries AD (see Chapter 5).

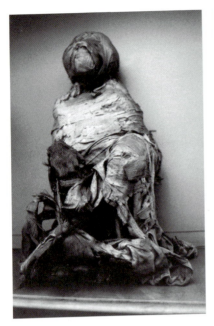

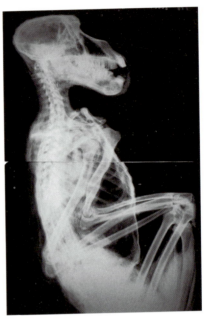

Animals as well as humans were mummified. This pet baboon was examined by X-ray radiography and some examples of veterinary practice are visible in the radiograph. Cairo Museum.

This X-ray shows that the baboon had injured its left humerus at some point during its life, and it has healed with only a slight bump. His canine teeth were removed to prevent him from inadvertently harming his owner. Cairo Museum.

A unique recipe for preserving bodies supposedly comes from the fourth century BC: immersion in honey. The most famous person who was supposedly preserved thus was Alexander the Great. Unfortunately, as Alexander's body is still lost to us there is no way of determining whether this is true or false. Certainly honey is a preservative and often used in food preservation (on hams and ducks), while a few other examples of it being used for humans are known.

There is an absence of information concerning mummies of the Christian or Coptic period. It appears that Christian mummies dating approximately from the fourth to sixth centuries AD were only cursorily cured using salt and occasionally natron. They were neither eviscerated nor excerebrated, and the use of resin and oils was limited. The arms invariably lay along the side of their bodies, and the mummies wore their own clothes, along with a winding sheet and shroud. An unusual Coptic mummy, now in the Graeco-Roman Museum in Alexandria, is elaborately wrapped with criss-cross bandages, reminiscent of pagan Roman mummies, save for the small black cross painted on the throat of the body. The paucity of Coptic mummies might be a result of the disapproval of early church notables of this custom as it had links with paganism. It is ironic, however, that, despite this, many important religious figures were embalmed after a fashion and buried within churches and monasteries, which are now sites of pilgrimages.

Fakes and restorations

During the process of mummification it was not unknown for various body parts to go missing. They would fall off as a result of over-desiccation or might even fall prey to dogs or rodents. In these cases the embalmer provided substitutes in the form of palm ribs, the bones of other animals and modelled mud. Bodies that showed signs of disease, such as the lady with bedsores (see above), would be restored to health for the Afterlife. The restoration of damaged mummies was also regarded as an act of piety, with the implication that the spirits of those whose burials had been restored would help one from the beyond. This was, no doubt, part of the reason why the royal mummies were carefully restored and reburied (see Chapter 7).

Even some non-royal mummies benefited from acts of piety. A mummy in the Manchester Museum (No. 1770) belongs to a fifteen-year-old girl. The wrapping style dates the mummy to the Ptolemaic period, but carbon-14 dates suggest that the mummy was older and that the Ptolemaic wrappings were a restoration. The body lacks its lower limbs, and fake wooden legs and feet were made as substitutes. The embalmers were unsure of the mummy's gender, so they provided it with nipple covers, as if she were female, and a false phallus, in case the mummy were male. Maybe the body was of an unknown individual and found in an advanced stage of decomposition when it was prepared. If it were of an unknown individual, the question of why it was so carefully prepared and bandaged arises. Perhaps the body had been found in the Nile, partly devoured by crocodiles, a fate that semi-deified an individual, and would explain the elaborate wrappings. Another Ptolemaic period burial, that of Isadora at Tuna el-Gebel, celebrates her deification through her death by drowning in the Nile. Certainly there are very few other understandable reasons for elaborate restorations of non-royal mummies.

The scientific study of mummies

Egyptologists now study mummies for the information that they can provide about the technology, religion, diet, familial relationships and diseases of ancient Egypt. In the past mummies were often unceremoniously unwrapped in order to see how they were mummified and to look upon the visages of the people of ancient Egypt. Now, however, mummies can be studied non-destructively by using highly scientific methods developed for doctors and medical research: X-rays, computerized tomography scanning, magnetic resonance imaging and tests of various types.

The non-destructive imaging of the bones and the tissues contained in the mummy bandages allows one not only to see body positions, and thus to plot changes in these over time, but also to determine disease, gender and age through the study of the bones. The soft tissue can be seen, and information about the evisceration and desiccation gathered from these images. Using these images scientists can even carry out facial reconstruction so that the features of the dead person are recreated and one can look upon their faces once again. Teeth have also been studied to provide information about the deceased's age, dental health and diet.

Tests have also been developed using mummified tissue to determine the presence of certain diseases such as malaria, schistosomiasis or bilharzia, and trichinosis, the last two of these being parasitic diseases. Work is being carried out to see whether smallpox and other diseases can be identified in mummies. Ramesses V is supposed to have suffered from smallpox as the remains of pustules can be seen on his face.

Other ailments have been found by examining mummies, from simple broken bones to various lung diseases. Several mummies, such as that of Nakht in the Royal Ontario Museum, and Nakhtankh in the Manchester Museum, suffered from anthracosis, a lung disease caused by inhaling smoke from fires and oil lamps in poorly ventilated places. Sand and dust inhalation, easily done in Egypt, can also cause similar diseases, such as pneumoconiosis or perhaps silicosis. Evidence of tuberculosis has also been found in ancient Egyptian mummies dating from the Predynastic period as well as from the Nineteenth and Twenty-first Dynasties. Leprosy has also been found in Egypt, primarily in the Ptolemaic period where some examples have been found in male burials. Furthermore, a possible case of poliomyelitis has been recorded in the pharaoh Siptah's mummy: he has one short and withered leg. On the other hand, the same symptoms can result from certain types of cerebral palsy; until tests are developed to determine the presence of either of these diseases in mummies, one can only conjecture as to the cause of Siptah's handicap. Arteriosclerosis, or calcification of the arteries, seemed to be a common complaint among pharaohs and commoners during all periods of Egyptian history, even as it is in the population of modern Egypt.

The possibility of DNA studies on mummies is also being explored. These studies would provide information on gender, family relationship, genetic and infectious diseases and, in the case of animals, species. So far only small portions of genetic information that are encoded in the DNA have been studied. DNA testing for mummies is in its infancy, and its full potential has yet to be explored and, indeed, determined. Thus far, no completely successful DNA samples have been recovered from ancient Egyptian mummified remains. Perhaps in the near future this will be possible, and many questions regarding the relationships of the royal families of Egypt will be answered.

Notes

[1] Source: Based on de Sélincourt, A. 1972. *Herodotus: The Histories*, revised by A. R. Burn. Harmondsworth: Penguin.

4
Animal mummies

The Egyptians mummified and buried not only humans but also animals. The number of mummified animals surpasses the number of mummified humans, by several millions. Animal mummies are of four varieties: beloved pets, buried with their owners or in individual graves; victual mummies, consisting of an eternal supply of food for the Hereafter for humans; sacred animals that were worshipped during their lifetime and mummified with pomp upon their death; votive mummies, dedicated as offerings at the shrines of specific gods to whom these animals were sacred. The first three types of animal mummies occur throughout Egyptian history; the last type dates predominantly to the later periods of Egyptian history.

Pet mummies

The most charming type of animal mummy is that of beloved pets. From the Old Kingdom onward, Egyptians are pictured in their tombs, and on stelae, with their pets, thus ensuring their continued joint existence in the Afterlife. Occasionally the pets would have their names carved above their image, providing further insurance for their eternal life. Some pet-lovers went so far as

These votive cat mummies are wrapped in a variety of ways and come from cemeteries all over Egypt. Cairo Museum, photograph by Anna-Marie Kellen.

Sloping "beds" were used for embalming and pouring libations over animal mummies, especially in the Late Period. The whole area is thickly encrusted with oils used on the ibis and baboon mummies prepared here. Tuna el-Gebel.

to bury their pets with them, and many of these burials survive until today. Other pets were buried near the tomb of their owner, in a separate sepulchre, complete with funerary equipment. The evidence suggests that the pets lived out their natural lives and were mummified on death. If they died before their owner, then they awaited his or her arrival in the tomb. Pets that died after their owner were probably buried in the vicinity of their owner's tomb if it had already been sealed.

Dogs are the earliest pets depicted on tomb walls and are frequently found mummified and entombed. A king's guard-dog, Abutiu, had a tomb, paid for by his owner, in Giza. The inscription in the chapel records that the king provided the dog not only with a tomb but a coffin, fine linen and incense, all things that would have been given to a high-ranking human. Hapy-min of Abydos (Dynasty XXX) was buried with his pet dog curled up at his feet, very much like the medieval tomb carvings of Europe, which featured the knight, his lady and their hounds. Inw-min of Asyut (Dynasty XII) might have also been buried with his dog, who is pictured and named on his coffin, although neither mummy was recovered by the excavators. Another Middle Kingdom canine burial is that of Aya. Aya was buried in a wooden coffin similar to those produced for humans, with a complete offering formula. Sadly, the name of his mistress is lost. A splendidly well-preserved dog found in the Valley of the Kings with some of his bandages still adhering to his paws might have belonged to King Amenhotep II.

Prince Djhutmose, eldest son of Amenhotep III, had a special limestone sarcophagus carved for his pet cat, Tamyt. The cat is shown before an offering table such as was placed before humans. Isetemkheb D, wife of the High Priest of Amun (Dynasty XXI), was buried with her pet gazelle who was wrapped in cloths from the royal household. Ankhshepenwepet's tomb (Dynasty XXV) also contained a gazelle. The area outside Senenmut's Theban tomb, No. 71 (Dynasty XVIII), contained the burials of a horse and a monkey. Both were wrapped, and the monkey was provided with a bowl of fruit to enjoy in the Hereafter. The mare, equipped with a saddle-cloth, showed signs of illness and must have been a cosseted pet to have been mummified and interred in a sarcophagus.

In the Valley of the Kings, tombs KV 50 and KV 51 were found to contain several mummies of baboons, the above-mentioned dog, and ducks. In the former someone had arranged the mummies so that in the corner of the tomb a baboon and a dog were looking at each other woefully. It is unclear whose pets these animals were, although King Amenhotep II has been suggested in view of the proximity of his tomb. An interesting feature of the baboons is that they all had their canines removed so that they would not inadvertently harm their owner. The God's Wife of Amun (i.e. a high ranking priestess), Maatkare, also had a pet

The coffin contains the elaborately bandaged and prepared body of a Dorcas gazelle. It was mummified in the same way that humans of the Twenty-first Dynasty were: the victual organs were returned to the body, and the body was "fleshed" out so that it looked alive. Cairo Museum, photograph by Anna-Marie Kellen.

monkey buried with her. Initial investigators of her burial mistook it for an illegitimate baby, and it was not until nearly a hundred years later that this slur on her virtue was removed when X-rays showed that the baby was actually a monkey.

At Heliopolis there is a Predynastic cemetery which contains tombs of small herbivores, perhaps gazelles, as well as dogs. These might be pets, or, conceivably, an early cemetery for an animal cult.

The majority of pet animals were mummified in a manner that was similar to that of humans. They were eviscerated, although

A hunting dog found in tomb 50 in the Valley of the Kings. It is eviscerated along the length of its belly. No wrappings remain, except on its paws. Cairo Museum, photograph by Anna-Marie Kellen.

the cut was not always in the left flank; it could be in the belly or through the anal area. Then they were desiccated with natron, or possibly salt, before being oiled, coated with resin and wrapped, often with amulets interspersed among the wrappings. Some of the animals, notably the baboons, had linen packets stuffed in their torsos so as to keep the shape of the animal intact.

Victual mummies

Victual, or food, mummies are perhaps the most unusual genre of animal mummy from ancient Egypt. Tutankhamun had over forty such cases of food mummies buried with him to feed him in the Afterlife. Most of these date from the necropoleis of the New

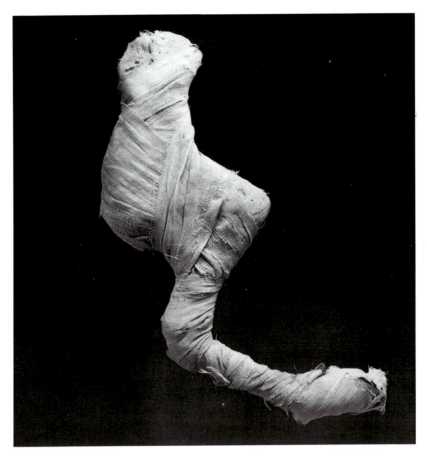

The left foreleg of a calf, provided as a food offering to Isitemkheb D. Cairo Museum, photograph by Anna-Marie Kellen.

Kingdom in Thebes, although the roots of this practice extend back to the Old Kingdom, and some examples from the Twenty-first Dynasty are also known. These mummies consist of joints of beef, and occasionally mutton, as well as whole birds (ducks, geese and pigeons) that have been prepared for roasting. The poultry is beheaded, its wing-tips and feet are removed, and eviscerated, with some of the viscera returned to the body, much as a modern supermarket chicken is prepared for cooking. Then the joints or poultry were "cured" using salt and, in some instances, crude natron. Recent tests have shown that in some instances a generous amount of vegetable oil was poured over the wrapped mummies – perhaps as a prelude to cooking them. Some mummies are coloured brown; it is possible that a roasted appearance (browning) was given to these mummies by the application of very hot resin on the wrapping which no doubt cooked the exterior surface of the mummy, while preventing bacterial infestation. Close investigation of these mummies would suggest, however, that it was more probable that the resin on the mummies came from the pitch or oil applied to the interior of the coffinets rather than to the mummies themselves. They are then bandaged, and put into wooden coffinets whose interiors are coated with resins to discourage insects and bacteria, and whose exteriors, in some cases, are covered with white plaster. Perhaps the white coating is meant to mimic the stone coffins used for food offerings in the Old and Middle Kingdoms.

One of the most unusual joints of meat in the Cairo Museum collection came from the burial of Isetemkheb D (Dynasty XXI) and comprised the lungs and windpipe of a young cow. This might be regarded not only as food but also as a symbol for the unified Egypt: the windpipe and lungs, with a knot tied over them by the lotus and papyrus plants, is the *sema-tawy*, a common symbol of unification pictured on royal thrones. Isetemkheb's victual mummies also included the tail of a young cow, which leads one to speculate that oxtail soup may have been on the menu in the next world.

Sacred animals

Animal cults were common in Egypt throughout its history, although they reached an acme of popularity in the Late and Graeco-Roman periods. Animal cults focused on one specific animal, in which the spirit (*ba*) of a specific god resided, and was worshipped as the manifestation of the god's power for the duration of the animal's lifetime. During its lifetime the animal was cared for and revered as if it were the god himself. These animal cults often had strong oracular components and allowed a certain amount of access to the god for the common people, a feature that was not common in most pharaonic Egyptian cultic ritual.

On the sacred animal's death it was mummified and buried in an elaborate tomb with many of the accoutrements provided for a king. The essence of the god's spirit would then be reborn in the body of another beast, recognizable by its markings, and, once it was identified by the priests, much as is done with each new Dalai Lama, it would take its place as the new manifestation of the god's divine essence on earth.

The best-known and most long-lived animal cults were the bull cults, often having solar connections. There were several such cults in Egypt, but the most important were the Apis bull, sacred to Ptah, at Memphis, the Mnevis bull of Re at Heliopolis and the Buchis bull of Montu at Armant. The dates of inception of these cults are unclear; there is evidence from the First Dynasty for the celebration of the cult of the Apis, if not before. The majority of evidence for these cults comes mainly from the New Kingdom onward. It is unknown when these cults died out; most survived into the Roman period. The Mnevis cult died out probably at some time in the early fourth century AD, along with the other bull cults. The Buchis cult definitely survived until AD 362, while the cult of the Apis bull was the last to survive until the Emperor Honorius banned it and caused the destruction of the Serapeum, the cult and burial place of the bull, in AD 398. However, it should be noted that the last certain burial there comes from the time of Cleopatra VII, over four centuries earlier.

The earliest intact Apis burial discovered dates to the reign of Horemheb in the New Kingdom. When the rectangular coffin containing the bull was opened, the mummy proved to be a surprise: it consisted solely of a bull's head, devoid of flesh and skin, resting on a large black mass. The dark mass, when examined, proved to be a bundle of resin, fragmentary bovid bones and pieces of gold leaf, all wrapped in fine linen. The canopics of the Apis bull seem to be filled with indeterminate resinous material.

Excavations under the floor of the burial chamber yielded a dozen large crude pottery jars, containing ashes and burnt bones. Similar jar-deposits were also present in a few other Apis tombs. This evidence has led some scholars to suggest that, during the New Kingdom at least, the sacred bull's body was cooked and eaten by the pharaoh and the priests before its interment as a means of absorbing its divine power. A connection has been suggested between this occurrence and the so-called "Cannibal Hymn" of the Pyramid Texts (Utterances 273–274), which speaks of the king devouring the gods to take on their powers. It is possible that this hypothesis has some truth in it, but it is also possible that there is some other explanation for this practice. Certainly, no other sacred animals were devoured by their former guardians.

Later Apis bulls were definitely fully mummified, and we know that a large embalming workshop for the bulls was constructed at Memphis during the Twenty-sixth Dynasty. A papyrus dating from that dynasty describes the method used to embalm an Apis bull, although the focus is less on the actual mummification, and more on the order of wrapping and the amulets that were to be included. There is some mention of both forms of mummification, with the conventional evisceration from a cut and the enemetic removal of the entrails, being employed, with the desiccation and wrapping procedures being standard. The canopic jars for the Apis and the Mnevis bulls that have been found would suggest that the more standard evisceration procedure was used on these animals. However, even the use of the turpentine method of voiding the body did not preclude the inclusion of canopic jars as a symbol of the absent internal organs. After all, canopic jars were included in human burials where the viscera had been returned to the body cavity. Embalming beds, or perhaps beds used for wrapping the bull, made of Egyptian alabaster, have been excavated at the site of Memphis where the Apis bull lived out its life.

The use of turpentine or juniper oil enemas for the mummification of large sacred animals seems to have been standard in the Late and Graeco-Roman periods, as this appears to have been the favoured

The mummified remains of a Mother-of-Apis from Saqqara. The cartonnage form contains the head of a cow. Cairo Museum, photograph by Anna-Marie Kellen.

method used when embalming a Buchis bull, a manifestation of the god Montu. Several Buchis bull burials from Armant have been found intact, most dating from the Late and Roman Periods. These burials provide more information about the mummification of cult animals, although this too is limited owing to the water-damaged state of the bodies. The discovery of large metal enemas and two bronze vaginal retractors (no doubt used for evisceration) indicate that the bulls (and their mothers who were also mummified) were eviscerated by rectally injecting them with juniper oil and plugging

A sacred ram from the cemetery at Elephantine. It is covered with gilded cartonnage, and amulets are scattered over its body. Cairo Museum, photograph by Anna-Marie Kellen.

up the orifice. As with the rabbit experiment mentioned in Chapter 3, the animals were then desiccated using natron. This procedure would no doubt take at least forty days if not longer, owing to the size of the animal. Once the viscera had softened, the animal would be squeezed, and the internal organs would exit from the anal orifice. The brains appear to have been left in place.

Once the bulls had been satisfactorily eviscerated and desiccated, they were wrapped. This was an elaborate operation that involved

Like human mummies, this hawk mummy has a mask. X-rays show that the bird is actually headless. Cairo Museum, photograph by Anna-Marie Kellen.

cutting the tendons of the hind-legs so that the bull could be made to kneel in a sphinx-like position without damaging the bones. The animal was then fastened to a wooden board with a series of metal clamps through which bandages were passed to secure the bull to the board, and then the creature was wrapped, as the relative position of bandages to board indicates. The tail was placed under the right hind leg. A wooden chin-rest supported the head, and the wrapped animal was covered by a shroud. The heads of the bulls were covered by masks embellished with gold leaf, and artificial eyes made of stone and glass. There are some other Late Period animal cults with cemeteries of mummified animals such as the Mothers of Buchis and Apis. Each burial contains an individual animal.

Other sacred animals include the ram god, Banebjedet, of Mendes, and the ram god, Khnum, of Elephantine. These animals were eviscerated, but it is not yet clear whether this was accomplished per anum or through a slit in the belly, as was used for pet animals. Amulets and bead nets frequently adorned these mummies whose heads were covered with gilded cartonnage masks. Often their heads maintained their upright positions by being reinforced by a wooden or cartonnage support.

Sacred crocodiles, incarnations of the god Sobek, some measuring over five metres, are among the most striking ancient Egyptian animal mummies. Sometimes more than one crocodile was mummified: the British Museum boasts a family group that was mummified together. A female, surmounted by a male, and surrounded by numerous baby crocodiles were all wrapped as a unit. Another similar group, from Lahun, strangely has the uppermost adult animal chopped into pieces. It is probable that the mature animals were thus juxtaposed to suggest mating and the infant crocodiles showed the fulfilment of this act, also underlining the idea of resurrection and rebirth that was associated with the solar nature of these animals.

Votive mummies

The largest number of animal mummies is a group that has long been termed votive mummies, numbering in the millions. The role of these mummified creatures is difficult to grasp, and scholars are still working to understand their precise role in Egyptian cults. These animals are not sacred in the same way as were the Apis bull or other beasts that served as a repository for a god's *ba*. One theory put forward is that they were consecrated in some way because they might have lived within the sacred precincts or were manifestations of the holy animals, although not the "chosen ones" themselves. Another hypothesis is that they served as votive offerings. These mummies were purchased by pilgrims from priests and were placed in catacombs dedicated to a specific god. These animals performed the same function that a lighted candle does in a church; they acted as the physical manifestation of a prayer addressed by the pilgrim to the divinity for eternity. Whether these animals served as specific offerings given by individuals, or were pious burials of animals that lived within the temple grounds, they were, to some extent, associated with divinity. Although the majority of the catacombs containing massive animal burials date to the Late and Graeco-Roman periods, the idea of divine association of animals goes back to the Predynastic period where ritual burials of animals, including cattle, elephants and baboons, have emerged from Naqada II and III levels at Hierakonpolis. However, there are few excavated mass animal cemeteries from the intervening periods of Egyptian history. It is not until the twilight of Egypt's history that animal cemeteries become common. Perhaps this is part of a harking back to earlier beliefs and is a manifestation of nationalism and an attempt to separate Egyptian religion in a country that had been ruled by Libyans, Nubians, Assyrians, Persians and Greeks.

By the end of Egyptian history a vast range of species had been mummified in some cult centre or another. These included cats, dogs, ibises, fish, raptors, scarab beetles, snakes, crocodiles, baboons, cattle, crocodile eggs and shrews. Classical authors even mention lion mummies at Saqqara; these have been rediscovered by Alain Zivie in his excavation at the Bubasteion.

An interesting feature about these mummies is that the animals did not all meet with natural ends. Unlike pets and sacred animals, votive mummies were not, for the most part, allowed the luxury of a natural death. Many of the cat mummies, found in the precinct of the feline divinity, Bastet, goddess of love, music and the more sensual of life's pleasures, had been deliberately killed so that they could be mummified. X-rays show that they were killed by having their necks broken, while others had their skulls crushed with a blunt instrument. They were then eviscerated, covered with crude natron to desiccate them and bandaged, with resins being applied to the bandages, and, in some cases, to the animal itself. Ibises, sacred to the god Thoth, god of wisdom and writing, and various raptors, sacred to solar deities, such as Horus, were mummified, but X-rays reveal nothing of how they died. It is possible that they died naturally, although some scholars have suggested that the live birds were dipped into boiling vats of resin or pitch and that is how they were mummified. Once the animals were mummified, they were then placed in the hypogea cut into either the cliffs or bedrock. Some of these animals were put into individual coffins, or several mummies were put into pottery jars (especially common for ibises), which were sealed and interred.

Other votive animals include young crocodiles (and in some cases crocodile eggs containing foetal crocodiles) that were dedicated to the god Sobek; these again do not show any marks of violence. Shrews, associated with solar deities, are also found, either singly, or in groups – often of fifteen or more. Again there is no way of knowing how they died, or indeed how these notoriously shy animals were captured.

The question of how these animals were collected is particularly intriguing. The vast number of these mummies (over 10,000 birds must have been interred at Saqqara annually) raises the question as to whether these animals were raised specifically for mummification on the site or whether they were collected from the entire country. This is an especially interesting question with regard to certain animals that do not breed well in captivity, such

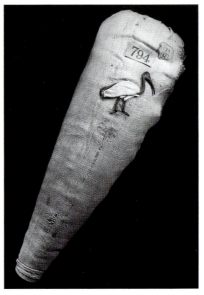

Coffered bandaging was very popular for both humans and animals at the end of the Ptolemaic period and in the Roman period. This wrapped bundle contains an ibis. Cairo Museum, photograph by Anna-Marie Kellen.

Although the packaging would suggest that this is an ibis mummy, radiographs show that it is a fake, stuffed with sand and mud. Cairo Museum, photograph by Anna-Marie Kellen.

as raptors. Perhaps this is why many mummy bundles that appear to be raptors actually contain only mud or only a fragment of a bird, with the idea that a part symbolizes the whole. Late Period mummies of raptors were commonly misidentified as mummies of children until they were unwrapped. This was because the embalmers wrapped the mummy with a lot of bandages so that it looked baby sized and covered the head area with a cartonnage mask (made of plaster-permeated linen and papyrus) of a human face. The use of a human mask ceased in the later part of the Graeco-Roman period. The percentage of faked raptor mummies far exceeds the fakes of other species. Some scholars have suggested that these fake mummies are not real "fakes" but, rather, the amalgamation of sacred detritus, similar to an embalmer's cache. However, this would beg the question as to why so much trouble was taken with the animal detritus, elaborately wrapping it into the form of a carefully bandaged mummy, while human detritus, including that of royalty, was unceremoniously bundled into jars and buried.

5
Funerary equipment and provisioning the dead

Preparing for death was a costly operation. Not only did one have to construct a tomb (Chapter 6), but one had to arrange for mummification and the equipping of the tomb.

Adorning the mummy: amulets, jewellery and other ornament

Preparing and wrapping the mummy was only part of the preparation of the body. A major component of the protection afforded the desiccated corpse came from the amulets and jewellery interspersed in the wrappings and, especially in later periods, ornaments that protected the exterior of the wrappings.

Amulets

An amulet is basically a charm, often inscribed with a spell, magic incantation or symbol, that protects the wearer against evil or provides aid and magical benefits. Amulets can aid or provide healing, luck, protection or even act as a double or replacement for an organ or limb. There are several ancient Egyptian words for

Blue faience amulets from the Late Period. Top to bottom: winged scarab flanked by smaller scarabs, djed pillar flanked by tyt amulets (top) and more djed pillars, menat (counterbalance), wadjet eye, and heart (ib) amulet. Cairo Museum.

amulet, most notably *sa* and *wedjau*. The former means amulet and is also very similar in sound to the word "protection". The latter has the same sound as the word meaning well-being and prosperity, and is probably related to it. A large variety of amulets were placed on the body and scattered among the wrappings to ensure the safety of the body and an easy passage into the Afterlife. A list of important funerary amulets from ancient Egypt actually appears in the MacGregor Papyrus. Both royal and non-royal individuals included amulets in their mummy bandages; Tutankhamun had over 140 amulets scattered through his wrappings. The "Book of the Dead" specifically mentions certain amulets that have magical obligations to the deceased, notably the headrest and *wadj* pillar, which should be included with the mummy.

An amulet's power comes from its shape, material and colour. Green and blue stones, glass or faience signified resurrection and rebirth; haematite was used for amulets providing strength and support; carnelian, jasper, red glass or red faience were used for any amulet that symbolized blood, energy, strength, power and solar force.

Although funerary amulets were important throughout Egyptian history, the type and number of amulets used changed over time. There were, however, certain amulets that were fairly standard throughout Egyptian history.

Perhaps the best known ancient Egyptian amulet is the *wadjet* eye, or eye of Horus. It is quite possible that, in modern Egypt, some Coptic and Islamic protective charms against the evil eye are derived from the *wadjet* eye. This amulet was supposed to represent the eye of Horus or of Re and protected the wearer against all evils by taking on the powers of the god. Amulets representing the eye are found all over the body, interspersed with the wrappings. From the New Kingdom onward, the incision for eviscerating the corpse was often covered subsequently with a wax or metal plate decorated with the *wadjet* eye.

The *djed* pillar was another favourite funerary amulet. The pillar is a symbol of Osiris, and has been interpreted as being part of his vertebral column, or even the trunk of a palm tree used as a column. It signifies endurance and stability. Chapter 155 of the Book of the Dead refers to it, and it was generally found on the mummy's throat as well as on the chest. A baboon mummy, now in the Mallawi Museum, has a *djed* pillar attached to its lower back, thus stressing its identification as Osiris's back. Most of these amulets are made of faience or of lapis lazuli. Another symbol indirectly associated with Osiris was the *wadj*, an amulet in the shape of a green papyrus stalk. This green stalk was associated with rebirth and regeneration, the making green of things, something that was part of Osiris's responsibilities. Especially from the New Kingdom onward the *djed* pillar was associated with the *tyt*. The *tyt* amulet, or Isis knot/girdle, symbolizes protection by the blood of Isis. Thus, it was made of red materials, and it also signified potential fertility and rebirth.

Heart scarabs, the classic mummy amulet, were introduced in the Middle Kingdom. This large scarab protected the heart of the deceased and served as a replacement should his own heart be destroyed. The extreme importance of the heart in the ritual of judgement, and the eventual arrival of the deceased in the Afterworld, ensured that the heart scarab was among the most crucial amulets on a mummy. The scarab was placed over the heart and its base was inscribed with texts from the Book of the Dead, notably Spell 30:

> O my heart which I had from my mother, O my heart which
> I had upon earth, do not rise up against me as a witness in the

presence of the Lord of Things; do not speak against me concerning what I have done, do not bring up against me anything I have done in the presence of the Great God, Lord of the West.

Scarabs, symbols of the sun god and resurrection, and derived from the beetle, *Scarabaeus sacer*, were also popular amulets. The Egyptians associated these dung beetles with resurrection after observing some of their habits. The beetle lays its eggs and wraps them up in a dung/mud ball, which provides the larvae with nourishment. To the Egyptians the ball of dung from which new life sprang was miraculous and rapidly associated with the sun-disc that goes across the sky and is reborn every day, and is identified with the new-born sun god, Khepri. Scholars have also suggested that scarabs are so closely identified with mummies because the beetle pupae resemble wrapped-up mummies. Furthermore, the egg-bearing dung ball is created in an underground chamber reached by a vertical shaft and horizontal passage, much like a tomb. Scarabs were not always in the form of just beetles. Human- and animal-headed scarabs have been found, with one of the most striking being the human-headed heart scarab of Sobkemsaf II of the Seventeenth Dynasty.

The *pesesh-kef* amulet was also a significant part of the corpus of funerary amulets. This amulet derives from the *pesesh-kef* knife set that was involved in the ritual of Opening of the Mouth (Chapter 7) and had its origins in the cutting of the umbilical cord and clearing the newborn infant's mouth of mucus so that it could breathe and eat, and thus facilitated the use of all one's senses in the Afterlife. These amulets are generally made of obsidian, basalt, steatite and serpentine. It is possible that these amulets evolved into or are confused with the two feather amulets (symbolizing Amun) found in the Late Period. The two fingers-amulets, generally made out of a dark stone, are also probably related to the *pesesh-kef* set with the fingers interpreted as the fingers used to clear the newborn's mouth. This amulet tends to be found on the left side of the pelvis, near the embalming

Tutankhamun's pendant in the form of a wadjet eye, flanked by the tutelary goddesses of Upper and Lower Egypt: Wadjet and Nekhbet. Cairo Museum.

incision. Another explanation for this amulet is that it represents the fingers of the embalmer who makes the visceral incision.

As the head of the corpse was of particular importance for its successful resurrection, specific amulets for the protection of the head were also part of the funerary paraphernalia. One such amulet is the *wrs* or head-rest. This amulet has been found under the deceased's head and is frequently made of haematite. It is featured in the Coffin Texts Spell 232 and in the Book of the Dead, Chapter 166, which consists of a spell that was often found inscribed on it. The spell on them read as follows:

> O N [the deceased], may they awaken your head at the horizon. Raise yourself, so that you may be triumphant against what is done against you, for Ptah has felled your enemies, and it is commanded that action be taken against those who would harm you ... Your head shall not be taken from you afterwards, your head shall not be taken from you forever.

Another amulet that protected the head was the hypocephalus which was placed beneath the mummy's head. These large circular amulets were inscribed with Spell 162 of the Book of the Dead ("Spell to cause to come into being a flame beneath a head of a spirit") and decorated with images of various deities including Amun-Re, Isis, Nepthys, Thoth, Re, Horus and his Four Sons. These amulets are made of a variety of materials, including stuccoed linen, papyrus and bronze.

The *ankh*, or hieroglyphic symbol for life, was also an amulet that was frequently found on mummies. It was often red, although it could be green or blue, and encapsulated the hope of eternal life for the mummy. Amulets in the shape of a blue lotus were also popular as these flowers were a quintessential symbol of rebirth and resurrection. The blue lotus rises out of the water as the sun rises in the sky; then, when the sun is at its zenith, the lotus opens its flower; as the sun continues its course through the horizon, the lotus closes its petals, and sinks down under the level of the water until it is reborn again with the sun on the following day. The god Nefertum is shown with his head emerging from a lotus as he is reborn; the famous sculpture from Tutankhamun's tomb is also a representation of this belief and was no doubt included in the tomb to ensure the young king's safe resurrection.

A host of other amulets appear on mummies throughout the long course of Egyptian history. These include amulets in the shape of the Anubis jackal, lions (symbolic of strength), *ka-* and *ba-*shaped amulets, *maat* feathers and amulets in the shape of deities such as Nepthys, Amun, Thoth, Horus and the Four Sons of Horus. Hieroglyphic symbols meaning eternity (*shen*), or good/beautiful (*nefer*), were also translated into amuletic form.

External ornamentation

From the end of the Old Kingdom onward a shroud invariably enveloped the mummy. This was frequently left plain, with some decoration appearing in the New Kingdom, and then again in the Third Intermediate Period and later. Another decorative element is sometimes introduced into the mummy wrappings of the Twenty-second Dynasty: bead nets. Bead net dresses were made of long cylindrical faience beads threaded into a lozenge pattern with faience amulets in the shape of winged scarabs and the Four Sons of Horus incorporated into the design and were generally found on the bodies of females at this time. Some extremely ornate examples have elaborate beaded designs such as faces worked into the garment itself. These nets were especially popular in the Twenty-fifth and Twenty-sixth Dynasties and after, when they became universal for both sexes. They allude to the night sky of Nut. These nets may have some connection with Old Kingdom textual references to net dresses, and actual two- and three-dimensional representations of them exist from this period. At least two actual examples of such net dresses have been excavated: one from Giza (G 7440Z), and another at the site of Qau. Divinities such as Isis and Nepthys, as well as Osiris, are depicted wearing such net dresses. Some of the sacred Rams from the

Some bead nets had elaborations in the form of faces, scarabs and even the Four Sons of Horus incorporated into the main netting. Cairo Museum.

animal necropolis at Elephantine are also covered with bead nets, reminiscent of the one worn by Osiris. Perhaps the net helped to identify the deceased with Osiris.

Gilded imitation cartonnage bandages (plaster-permeated linen and papyrus, rather like papier mâché) are another decorative feature found on mummies at certain periods, such as in the late Eighteenth Dynasty and Late Period. These mimic the lateral bandages used to hold the shroud in place, which are also shown on the exterior of Eighteenth Dynasty coffins. They are placed over the bandaged mummy, below the shroud, and often inscribed with spells. In the Ptolemaic period these external elements include a collar, an apron over the legs and boots or greaves. These all served to protect and enhance the wrapped mummy.

Gold finger-stalls were used to prevent the extremities from falling off, especially in royal burials, such as these that date to the Dynasty XXI burials at Tanis. Cairo Museum.

Hand and foot covers

The extremities of mummies were always fragile after desiccation, so protective finger- and toe-stalls were developed. These objects, frequently made of gold, appear on high-status burials of the New Kingdom and later. They helped to keep these extremities from breaking off and being lost. Further protection was provided by "clothing" made of precious metals. Sandals of solid gold adorned the feet of the mummies of Tutankhamun and Shoshenq II. A pair of tiny silver gloves were found in the Valley of the Kings (tomb KV 56) and seem to have once protected the hands of an infant princess. Such gloves have been found on other mummies: for example, one (belonging to Lord Londesbrough) which was unwrapped in the nineteenth century by Samuel Birch, was similarly adorned. On some poorer mummies, such as the early Third Intermediate Period Lyons mummy, the hands were bound up in linen so as to imitate gloves.

Jewellery

From the Predynastic period onward the Egyptian dead were provided with jewellery, be it made of shells, ceramic beads or gold

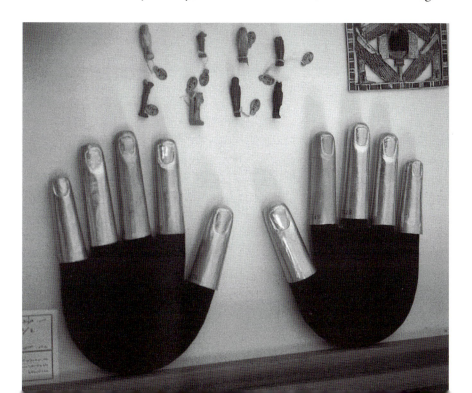

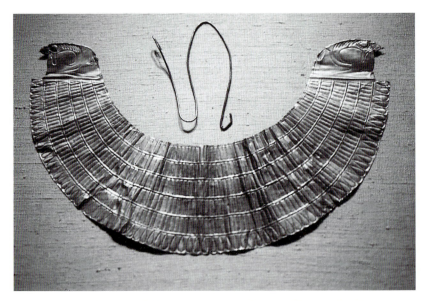

A collar made of thin gold foil with its two ends shaped as hawks. Because of its thinness scholars believe that it was used exclusively as funerary jewellery. Metropolitan Museum of Art.

and semi-precious stones. Jewellery adorned the corpse itself as well as being included in the funerary equipment. Two categories of jewellery have been found on mummies. The first comprises items made specifically for the burial, and the second is jewellery used during the lifetime of the deceased.

Burial jewellery can be differentiated from real jewellery by its flimsy construction. It is often cut from thin sheets of gold and is partially amuletic in function. The most common types of such ornaments are collars of hammered and incised, or stamped, gold in the shape of the protective vulture or cobra goddesses, *Wadjet* and *Nekhbet*. Gold bands for wrists or ankles were also produced. Good examples come from the tomb of Tutankhamun. This type of jewellery provides an economical alternative for the deceased and his family.

"Real" jewellery is jewellery actually worn during the deceased's lifetime and is solid and wearable. All sorts of objects, ranging from rings to neck-ornaments, anklets and bracelets are included in this category. This jewellery is part of the provisioning of the tomb, so that the deceased can enjoy all the delights of this world in the next.

Masks

Mummies of the early Old Kingdom have their facial features modelled in plaster over the surface of the bandages. At the end of the Old Kingdom, however, masks appear which were used to cover the head and shoulders of the mummy, serving to protect as well as to identify the deceased. Some of these were inscribed with spells that would further protect the head and shoulders of the mummy. Masks become particularly common from the Middle Kingdom onward and were made of plaster, wood or cartonnage. On rare occasions, they were fabricated from solid gold.

Although masks were supposed to represent the people that they cover, there was a certain standardization, especially in the less wealthy examples. However, individual features such as beards are frequently shown in paint. Royal examples tend to be better made and have a more recognizable portrait component. It is not until the Roman period, between the mid-first century AD and the third century AD, that a clear element of portraiture emerged in mask decoration.

In the Roman period "mummy portraits", often using the wax encaustic technique, were painted on wooden panels. These depict a slightly idealized, but compelling, portrait of the deceased, with clearly datable elements such as hairstyles, jewellery and elements of clothing. These would be placed over the face in the outermost layer of bandages. These panels are often known as Fayum portraits, as the first excavated examples came from the sites in that area, although they have subsequently been found all over Egypt. Mummy portraits are also sometimes painted on linen shrouds that are reinforced with a thin layer of plaster.

A Middle Kingdom cartonnage mask painted with the bearded features of the deceased. The paint on the tip of the nose has worn off from where it was in contact with the coffin lid. Cairo Museum.

The gilded funerary mask of Thuyu (Dynasty XVIII; KV 46) is enhanced with inlaid glass decorations. Cairo Museum.

The majority of non-royal masks are made of cartonnage, while the few royal examples that have survived are of precious metals. However, the faces of some of the non-royal examples are sometimes gilded. This probably provides an element of richness to the burial and, more importantly, alludes to the divine state achieved by the deceased in the Hereafter. In Egyptian religion, the flesh of the gods was of gold, their bones were of silver and their hair was of lapis lazuli. Gold on the mask evoked the transfigured state of the deceased. In the Roman period the actual desiccated faces of some mummies were gilded directly, as is illustrated by a head in the Petrie Museum.

Mummy boards

Until the end of the Eighteenth Dynasty, mummy masks ended at the collar. However, hands were then added, together with a separate cartonnage "openwork" covering the torso and legs, the latter derived from the gilded bands mentioned above. The two elements – hands and torso openwork – then fused together to become the mummy board. The mummy board covered the full length of the mummy and was made of carved wood, which was then plastered and painted. Boards are found from the Nineteenth to the early Twenty-second Dynasty. Some early Nineteenth Dynasty examples show the deceased as dressed and alive, but most are decorated in the same way as coffins of that period. Later Roman mummy portraits are somewhat reminiscent of the mummy boards that show the deceased as if alive. These mummy boards later gave way to all-enveloping cartonnage cases that were painted with a selection of funerary motifs.

These cartonnage cases, a cross between an extended mummy board and a coffin (see below), were features of Twenty-second Dynasty burials, and they replace mummy boards after the reign of Osorkon I. These coverings probably originated in the north of Egypt. They are generally painted and are decorated with brightly coloured mythological vignettes, images of the Four Sons of Horus and various protective winged deities. Yellow varnish is sometimes painted over the vignettes as protection, which does alter their final colour. These "body-gloves" were made out of plaster and linen (cartonnage), constructed over a "shape" made of mud and straw, which was removed once the case had dried. The cases are open at the back and under the feet, and the mummy was inserted into the case through these apertures. They were sealed by being laced up the back, and a board was inserted under the feet. Such a practice remained broadly standard until the middle of the Ptolemaic Period, although the ones from that period are recognizable in their liberal use of pink paint.

Fayum mummy portraits showed the deceased as in life. The details of hairstyle, jewellery and clothing help to date these portraits and provide information about their rank and status. This heavy-faced wealthy woman has a hair-pin stuck through her curls and is wearing pearl earrings and several necklaces. Cairo Museum.

Protecting the mummy: coffins and sarcophagi

Coffins

One of the most important articles of funerary equipment was the coffin. Coffins contained and protected the mummy. Their origin is rooted in the myth of Osiris. The chest that Seth had made to trap Osiris served as the prototype for coffins, and subsequent coffins owed their design to it. The fact that the chest was made of wood from the sycamore tree is why that wood was preferred for coffin manufacture, although wealthy individuals opted for cedar whenever possible. Cedar not only was an expensive imported wood but also was sweet smelling, discouraged bacterial growth and insect infestations and was linked to the Osiris myth as his coffin became lodged in that tree. Another reason for the use of sycamore wood is that the goddess Hathor, in her guise of the Lady of the Sycamore, provisioned the dead: thus anything made of that tree could be seen to sustain the deceased.

Ancient Egyptian coffins evolved over time, although they maintained two basic forms, rectangular (*qersu* in Egyptian) and anthropoid (*suhet* in Egyptian), which varied depending on the period of their manufacture. The former were almost always made of wood, while the latter could also have been of stone, cartonnage or gold. Cartonnage coffins are different from the cartonnage cases mentioned above as they have separate lids and troughs (the lower portion that contained the body).

Coffin design and decoration changed to accommodate evolving ideas of the Afterlife and were possessed of a very complex iconography. This is especially true for the Third Intermediate Period, when the decorations on the coffin supplanted the decorations in the tomb, and the decorated coffin was more the house for the mummy than was the tomb.

A coffin, or a nest of coffins, was frequently placed inside a sarcophagus. The word "sarcophagus" comes from the Greek for "flesh-eater", apparently from a Hellenic belief that some stones used for body containers actually consumed their contents. Sarcophagi are made of wood (sycamore, cedar, acacia) as well as stone (limestone, Egyptian alabaster, quartzite, granite or basalt) and served as further protection for the body. The Egyptian term for sarcophagus, *neb ankh*, means the "lord of life" and is indicative of the powers that were ascribed to it. Sarcophagi are almost invariably rectangular, while coffins can be rectangular or anthropoid.

This Old Kingdom granite sarcophagus from the tomb of Akhethotep at Giza shows architectural features carved onto the stone in relief. Brooklyn Museum, photograph by A. M. Dodson.

Old Kingdom coffins and sarcophagi

Predynastic burials did not include formal coffins, although there are some examples of baskets and large pottery jars being used to contain dead bodies. Early Dynastic wooden coffins are rectangular and relatively short as the body was buried in a flexed position. Many of these coffins are decorated with the "palace-façade" motif. This design represents the mudbrick panelled exterior of a dwelling, thus communicating the idea of the coffin as a house for the deceased. The lids of these coffins are either flat or vaulted, the latter design being reminiscent of the roofs of the shrines from Lower Egypt. The majority of Old Kingdom coffins are rectangular and relatively plain, with, from the Fourth Dynasty on, the only decoration being a line of offering-text that ran around the upper part of the box. A vertical line of text was added to the top of the lid as well. Later on a pair of eyes was added below the text that encircled the box, so that the deceased, who was buried on his or her side, could look out to the east and the land of the living. The habit of adorning the interior of the coffin began at some point in the Sixth Dynasty, with lists and representations of various offerings, objects and a false door (see Chapter 6) being added in paint. These representations presumably served to provision the dead in the Afterlife and must have played a part in the funerary rituals.

Stone sarcophagi are known from the Third Dynasty onward and were carved for both royalty and high officials at this time. They were made from Egyptian alabaster, limestone and granite. Most Old Kingdom sarcophagi were similar in form to coffins of the period: they were rectangular, although a unique oval sarcophagus was found in the Fourth Dynasty pyramid at Zawiyet el-Aryan. The sarcophagi were decorated with the palace-façade motif and had domed lids. Single lines of text were sometimes inscribed along the upper part of the rectangular trough. A few sarcophagi of this period display an unusual decoration on top of the domed lid: a stretched-out leopard skin is carved in bas relief. This might be an allusion to the night sky or to the various rituals the *sem*-priest (funerary priest) carried out on behalf of the deceased. It might even be connected to the occupation of the deceased in his life on earth.

Middle Kingdom coffins and sarcophagi

The rectangular coffin was generally favoured during the Middle Kingdom. The decoration of coffins from this period changed dramatically over time. The amount of exterior decoration increased to two or more lines of text running along the upper part of the box, augmented by four vertical bands of text on the long side of the rectangular coffin. These texts augment the horizontal offering texts and proclaim the importance of the deceased before various deities. False doors appear beneath the eyes so that the mummy can not only look out but receive offerings from the living. The interior also sometimes mirrored this false door. The

Middle Kingdom coffins, such as that of Sepet's from Deir el Bersheh, were decorated with object friezes as well as Coffin Texts, so that the deceased was well equipped for eternity. Louvre, photograph by A. M. Dodson.

exterior of richer coffins of this period was enhanced with gold foil and faience that imparted a rich and jewel-like appearance to these coffins.

By the end of the First Intermediate Period the interior walls and sometimes even the lids of coffins were decorated with "Coffin Texts" written in hieratic (Chapter 2) and the "Book of Two Ways". Frequently, the floor of the coffin, which lay directly beneath the mummy, was decorated with elaborate maps of the Underworld so that the deceased could safely negotiate a passage to the Hereafter. The "frieze of objects" also adorned the interior of the coffin, running along the four interior sides of the coffin. This frieze showed images of objects that were of both ritual and

A Dynasty XVII rishi coffin from Thebes showing the typical feathered pattern extending all the way down the body. Museum of Fine Arts, Boston.

practical significance for the deceased, ranging from sacred oils to bags of natron, shoes, weapons, furniture, jewellery and emblems of royalty that associated the deceased with Osiris. They are logically arranged so that they could be easily accessed by the deceased: head-rest at the head, jewellery and weapons near the arms, sandals at the foot, etc. Mirrors, symbolic of the sun and sources of a reflection of this life (thus an image of the Afterlife), started to play a significant role in funerary beliefs at this time and were pictured as an important part of the object frieze. The increased emphasis on the decoration of the interior of the coffin indicates that this was important from the deceased's perspective: the magic that was on the inside of the coffin was there to be absorbed and used by him or her.

Another text, invoking the sky goddess Nut, often appears along the inside of the lid. The location of this text is significant as it associates the lid of the coffin with the sky, whose length the sun traverses and is reborn daily, just as the deceased hopes to be reborn. The protective arch of the sky goddess encompasses the deceased and keeps him or her safe. Later coffins are actually decorated with an image of Nut on the underside of the coffin lid.

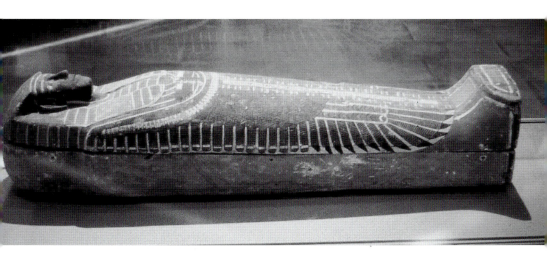

Anthropoid coffins were also developed during the Middle Kingdom. Conceptually, these seem to have been fully enveloping versions of the cartonnage masks that started to gain popularity in the First Intermediate Period. The coffin of Queen Aashayet (Dynasty XI) is the earliest such example of this trend. These anthropoid coffins represent the white-shrouded mummy wearing a mask (often coloured black as a symbol of resurrection and fertility) and a false beard (symbol of divinity) and are sometimes decorated with painted collars and bands of text evocative of the bandages used to hold the shroud in place. Later examples were polychrome or even entirely black. The anthropoid cases of the Middle Kingdom were placed within a rectangular coffin, lying on their left-hand (close to the heart) sides, thus indicating that the rectangular coffin acted as the tomb to the anthropoid coffin that protected the body of the deceased, like another layer of wrappings.

True independent anthropoid coffins developed during the Seventeenth Dynasty in the Second Intermediate Period. These show the deceased's face, ears, neck (embellished by a collar) and feet, but the rest of the coffin is decorated with feathers (*rishi*, in Arabic, which gave the name *rishi*-coffin to this type), which made it appear as if the deceased was enfolded by a giant bird. This might allude to the protection afforded the deceased as Osiris by Isis and Nepthys in their bird (kite) forms or might even suggest that the deceased had successfully become a *ba*: a human-headed bird. *Rishi*-coffins were used by kings until the Twenty-first Dynasty, but non-royal individuals gave them up early in the Eighteenth Dynasty in favour of other variations. The royal examples were often gilded or otherwise enhanced, while those belonging to non-royal individuals were merely painted.

Sarcophagi of Dynasty XI reflect some of the changes seen in coffins of the Middle Kingdom. The limestone sarcophagi belonging to the female members of Mentuhotep II's family are particularly interesting. They are not all made out of one piece of stone but of separate slabs jointed together. They are also decorated both inside and out. The interior decoration, executed in paint, is unlike the painted decoration of other coffins of the same period that pertains to the Hereafter. Rather, the interior of the sarcophagi is painted with scenes showing daily life activities, similar to those found depicted on tomb walls (Chapter 6). The exteriors of the sarcophagi are furthermore carved with daily life scenes, as well as the more standard iconography, such as mirrors (invoking the Hereafter), false doors and eyes.

Twelfth Dynasty sarcophagi are, in contrast, surprisingly plain. Many are completely undecorated, while some revert to the Old Kingdom models and have some exterior decoration in the form of the niched palace-façade; those of the late Twelfth Dynasty were apparently directly modelled on the enclosure wall of Djoser's Third Dynasty Step Pyramid at Saqqara.

New Kingdom coffins and sarcophagi

Rishi- and rectangular coffins ceased being used by non-royal individuals by the middle of the Eighteenth Dynasty, when they were supplemented by anthropoid coffins that are reminiscent of those dating to the Twelfth Dynasty. These were coloured white, with longitudinal and transverse bands in yellow. The wig is usually black, and the face is in the conventional male/female colours of red for males and yellow for females.[1] The trough is sometimes further enhanced with scenes of the deceased receiving offerings, mourners and the voyage to Abydos, depicted between the text bands.

This type of white coffin, and the very last *rishi* examples, was superseded by black anthropoid coffins. These coffins are found throughout the Eighteenth Dynasty and into the early Nineteenth Dynasty. As its sobriquet implies, the dominant colour is black, derived from the thick resinous varnish (in some instances resin, in others bitumen) that was applied to the surface of the wood. The face, headdress, horizontal and vertical bands of inscription and images of funerary deities interspersed among the

This typical black coffin from Thebes depicts an eye on the shoulder and the Four Sons of Horus, with relevant texts, on the rest of the coffin. The decoration is painted yellow to imitate gold. Royal Ontario Museum.

A pair of white coffins from the Theban tomb of Harmose (Dynasty XVIII, Thebes). The coffins are simply divided into sections by yellow bands that imitate the bandages that would keep the wrappings secure. Metropolitan Museum of Art.

lines of text and at the feet of the coffin were not coloured black, but yellow, indicative of gold or the colour of the sun. Some such coffins had a layer of yellowish varnish applied to the text (this varnish features in coffins of other periods as well). The verb "to varnish" in Egyptian is *senetjer*, which can also be translated as a word associated with incense (a key element of the mummification process), meaning "to make divine". Thus, the varnish helps transform the deceased into an eternal and divine being. Some of these coffins are also embellished by a red line painted at the junction of the two halves of the coffin: red, symbolic of strength and power, might have been placed here to magically fortify the weakest part of the coffin, and was also apotropaic. Wealthy individuals might also have had the yellow paint applied to their coffins' faces and the texts and figures replaced by gold foil. A few individuals also had a nest of up to three coffins, the innermost distinguished by being not "black" but entirely covered in gold. On the inner coffins, sometimes *djed* and *tyt* amulets were clasped in the hands of the deceased, and lotus blossoms adorned their legs.

Some important individuals of the Eighteenth Dynasty, following the reign of Amenhotep III, used stone rather than wood for their coffins. Basalt and granite were used, in addition to the softer limestone. These coffins mirrored the design of contemporary wooden ones and sometimes were only used as the outer coffin, although Merymose, the Viceroy of Nubia, has a nest of three stone coffins. The use of such stone containers continued into the Nineteenth Dynasty, with some early examples showing the deceased in his daily attire, rather than as a mummy. In this they imitated some contemporary mummy boards and certain wooden coffins. The decoration of both the coffins and sarcophagi of the periods continued to use portions of the Books of the Underworld.

The main trend in coffin development during the Ramesside Period was that of the "yellow" coffin, first found during the reign of Amenhotep III and ubiquitous by the early Nineteenth Dynasty. These have texts and funerary figures in polychrome, on a yellowish background, and are usually covered with a layer of varnish. Such coffins are datable by the density and complexity of their decorative texts and vignettes. The latter rapidly multiplied, with the small number of deities seen during the Eighteenth Dynasty proliferating considerably.

Pottery coffins, similar in spirit to those from the Predynastic period, are also found in the New Kingdom, and on through the Roman period. The New Kingdom examples are also called "slipper" coffins, as they were largely made in one piece, with a removable face and chest to permit the insertion of the body. Some are finely made, and even painted in the same way as wooden coffins. The later examples tend to be less well made and unpainted.

New Kingdom royal coffins retain a separate style from their non-royal counterparts. At the beginning of the Eighteenth Dynasty enormous cartonnage *rishi*-coffins were used for the huge outer coffins of royal women. Some of these, measuring well over three metres in length, were constructed from cartonnage laid over a wooden frame. Because of their size and mode of construction, the entire lid of the coffin did not lift off: only the portion above the waist was removable. Cartonnage coffins were shortly replaced by nests of wooden ones, some made of imported cedar. The carving and painting of these coffins is exquisite, showing each filament of individual feathers. Royal *rishi*-coffins developed so that the feather pattern was inlaid with pieces of gold, glass or semi-precious stone, making the entire coffin gleam and glitter like some exotic bird. The innermost coffin of Tutankhamun is made entirely of gold, and one can only imagine the appearance of royal coffins belonging to more important kings.

The outermost coffins of royalty changed in design during the reign of Seti I, when they began to be made of stone. Their decoration also changed and featured portions of various books of the Underworld. The preferred stone was Egyptian alabaster, a luminous white stone that invoked purity and light, although greywacke was also used as can be seen in the coffin of Ramesses VI.

This Dynasty XXI coffin belonged to Pediamun. It has the typical yellow background and the division into fields of decoration that is typical of that period. Luxor Museum of Mummification, photograph by A. M. Dodson.

There seem to be fewer private sarcophagi in the New Kingdom than in previous periods. In contrast to earlier periods, rectangular stone outer-cases made to hold the coffin only feature in the burial outfits of a handful of exceptional individuals, such as Hatshepsut's "favourite", Senenmut. The three or four that exist vary in shape, although this generally remains rectangular. They are decorated with Isis kneeling at the foot of the box, and Nepthys at the head, with the Four Sons of Horus appearing along the sides. The vast majority of private sarcophagi of the New Kingdom, even of royal in-laws, are of wood, and follow the coloration of the coffins that they were intended to contain, and are thus "black" or "yellow" in style, with eyes on both the lid and the box.

Royal sarcophagi of the New Kingdom initially took the form of a rectangular box with texts decorating its interior and exterior. The texts quote prayers uttered by funerary divinities, who are pictured in the frames created by the lines of text. Images of Nepthys and Isis protect the head and foot respectively. This basic form was embellished by carving a cartouche or *shen* on the lid. This magically ensured that the name of the deceased would endure through eternity.

The sarcophagus shape evolved from a rectangular box into a cartouche-shaped container, thus enclosing the body within eternity. Both inside and outside the sarcophagi, Isis and Nepthys retained their positions at head and foot, to protect the dead ruler. These sarcophagi continued to sport a pair of eyes on the side so the king could look out. Amenhotep III added a pair of eyes to the lid of his sarcophagus so that the king could see out while lying on his back. From the reign of Akhenaten until the end of the Eighteenth Dynasty, royal sarcophagi revert to a rectangular shape, with four protective figures on the corners. For Akhenaten, these are his wife Nefertiti, a living goddess, but Tutankhamun, Ay and Horemheb have the traditional images of the four protective goddesses, Isis, Nepthys, Neith and Selqet. Ramesses I once again had a cartouche-shaped sarcophagus, but the tombs of Seti

I and Ramesses II show no evidence of stone sarcophagi. This coincides with the adoption of stone outer coffins, which were perhaps paired with wooden sarcophagi.

This trend toward simplicity was reversed by Merenptah, who had three sarcophagi, as well as a stone coffin. The pairing of a cartouche-form sarcophagus – now with a recumbent figure of the king on the lid – and a stone coffin is then standard until the middle of the Twentieth Dynasty. Sarcophagus decoration changes dramatically, with portions of the Books of the Underworld being carved both on and in the sarcophagi of this time.

The Third Intermediate Period

Wooden anthropoid coffins (generally a pair), painted yellow (hence the name "yellow" coffin), and covered with dense poly-chrome decoration, are common at the start of the Third Intermediate Period. The decoration on the lids runs along the length of the body and consists of an elaborate floral collar, hands shown in raised relief, thin lines of text and scenes of various winged deities and funerary divinities dispersed over the body of the coffin. Early in the Twenty-second Dynasty a thin pair of crossed red braces are shown lying over the floral collar. The size of the latter gradually increased until it reached to the waist. The vignettes adorning the coffins relate to resurrection and the god-dess Nut. The trough of the case showed scenes found in the Book of the Dead and tomb paintings, including the judgement scene, Hathor as a cow emerging from a mountain, the deceased obtaining sustenance from the Goddess of the Sycamore and scenes illustrating various creation myths. The interiors of the coffins were also highly decorated. The lid of the coffin showed Nut stretched over the deceased, thus enclosing him in her pro-tective embrace. A *djed* pillar painted on the floor supported the back of the deceased, and a *ba*, hovering over the mummy's head, manifested the deceased's transformed state. The inner walls of

the coffins were covered by deities associated with the sun god. Another change in the coffin decoration of this period is the appropriation of the Amduat by non-royal individuals. Prior to Dynasty XXI the Amduat only appeared in royal contexts; however, at the start of the Third Intermediate Period its use was usurped by non-royals.

During the course of the early Twenty-second Dynasty, these yellow coffins vanish and are replaced by much plainer coffins with restrained decoration. Unlike the yellow coffins, which were of Theban origin, it is thought that these simpler coffins developed in the Delta. These coffins were mummiform, but only the face was defined; the hands had completely disappeared. Many of the coffins' exteriors were very simply decorated on a wooden or wood coloured background with a broad collar and bands of texts, and the interiors embellished only with a figure of Nut. Some enjoyed more elaborate decoration with the image of the god, Sokar-Osiris, and a series of winged divinities soberly dispersed over the coffins' exterior in muted colours, or even in cream on black. Solar imagery was commonly used during this period. In the Twenty-third Dynasty, images of Nut proliferate on the interior of the coffin.

The Twenty-third Dynasty saw a change in coffin shape which reflected a change in how the deceased was viewed. The coffin is mummiform but is placed on a pedestal, as if the mummy had been converted into an image that was mounted on a base. It is supported by a pillar along the back, just as is found in statuary. Once again, the deceased is transformed into an image of a *sah*. The pillar was painted with a *djed* and emphasized the deceased's relationship with Osiris. The front of these coffins shows the deceased wearing a broad collar and protected by winged deities. However, the salient decorative feature of these coffins is the vast amount of text in comparison with vignettes. The majority of the texts were taken from the Book of the Dead. This coffin type continued into the Twenty-fifth and Twenty-sixth Dynasties.

Harkhebi's basalt coffin from his tomb at Saqqara is typical of the Twenty-sixth Dynasty in its large, squat proportions and beautifully carved inscription. Metropolitan Museum of Art, photograph by A. M. Dodson.

In addition to existing coffin types that had evolved over time, Twenty-fifth and Twenty-sixth Dynasty burials also contained coffins that were deliberately archaizing. Coffins similar to the Middle Kingdom anthropoid coffins (but differentiated from the originals by pedestals and over-large collars) became common, and in some other anthropoid coffins the faces are painted green. Other rectangular coffins with vaulted lids and four upstanding posts at the corners also became popular at this time and remained so until the end of the Roman period.

Coffins for rulers initially retained the *rishi* design, although by the Twenty-second Dynasty they were once more synchronized with those of non-royal individuals. The only exception to this was the treatment of the face, which became that of a falcon, no doubt alluding to the falcon-headed god Sokar-Osiris. The use of silver as opposed to gold in royal burials is a feature of the Third Intermediate Period. Certain rulers also used stone coffins; these were generally usurped from the New Kingdom. The royal falcon-head seems to appear in some non-royal burials as well, perhaps after being discarded by kings in the reign of Pimay. Fragments of royal coffins that have been found from the end of the Twenty-fifth Dynasty may indicate a reversion to the *rishi* style, perhaps an archaic practice favoured by Egypt's then Nubian rulers.

Stone sarcophagi were not used by non-royal individuals in the Third Intermediate Period, while wooden ones remain unknown until the late Twenty-second Dynasty. These are rectangular in form with posts at the corners and arched tops. Stone sarcophagi were, however, favoured by royalty. Many of the royal examples were actually reworked sarcophagi from earlier periods, embellished with the names and titles of the new owners, in addition to carvings from religious texts. Some of the Twenty-second Dynasty rulers actually carved their own sarcophagi: Osorkon II and Shoshenq III were both buried in granite sarcophagi with rounded heads, and their lids were adorned by a mummiform figure carved in very low relief.

The Late Period and the Graeco-Roman Period

The vogue for stone coffins was revived in the Late Period and continued into the Ptolemaic era. Large anthropoid coffins, decorated only with a few simple lines of text and a broad collar, are typical of the period. The proportions of wooden coffins change, becoming more 'top-heavy', with large wigs and chest areas contrasting with squatter leg dimensions. The back pillar and pedestal continue to be a feature, sometimes in both the inner and the outer coffins. The decoration was also simplified, featuring Nut, scenes of the deceased on a lion-headed funerary bed, scarabs and solar discs. The texts tend to be sloppily written, filled with scribal errors. Rectangular, densely decorated coffins with posts emerging from four sides and covered by a domed lid are also common throughout this era. Finally, in the Roman Period, traditional anthropoid coffins tend to disappear, and bodies are usually covered with a cartonnage body casing and, if they are wealthy enough, a wooden sarcophagus. These cartonnage cases were made less often of linen and plaster but more frequently of papyrus, plaster and mud. The decorations are a mixture of classical and Egyptian motifs, exemplifying the religious synthesis typical of the period.

Canopic equipment

During mummification the viscera were removed from the body to be mummified separately. From the Fourth Dynasty on, special containers were made for the internal organs, which were called canopic boxes or chests. The term "canopic" is derived from a misunderstanding that occurred in the Greek period when the visceral jars were confused with a manifestation of Osiris, depicted as a human-headed jar, worshipped at the site of Canopus, a city that was named after Menelaeus's pilot. There is no specific known ancient Egyptian term for these containers; they are known as *qebu en wet*, or "jars of embalming". Generally, these were placed near the foot of the mummy, sometimes in a specially constructed niche within the tomb.

The canopic jars acquired individual heads in the New Kingdom, one for each Son of Horus. Bolton Museum.

A wooden shabti box containing shabtis that are painted blue, belonging to Pinudjem I (Dynasty XXI). Cairo Museum.

The earliest such container dates to the Fourth Dynasty burial of Queen Hetepheres, the mother of King Khufu. It took the shape of a plain square box made of Egyptian alabaster, divided into four compartments and covered by a lid. Later in the same dynasty another type of container came into use: a plain jar. Groups of four of these jars with flat lids are found as canopic receptacles in later tombs of Dynasty IV. Wooden chests divided into four were commonly used in non-royal burials; sometimes the chests contained separate vessels for the viscera.

In the Middle Kingdom the lids of canopic jars adopted the appearance of human heads, and remained thus until the New Kingdom. Some visceral bundles that are not placed in jars are covered with cartonnage masks with human faces, such as those found on the deceased. An unusual cartonnage canopic container made for Djehutynakht of Bersha is in the shape of a person with legs and feet. Similarly, the calcite canopic jars for King Senusert I have arms hanging down by their sides. Prior to this time the inscriptions on canopic jars or chests (or both) listed the name and titles of the deceased. However, during the Middle Kingdom each internal organ was put under the protection of one of the Four Sons of Horus: the liver was under the protection of Imseti, the lungs under Hapy, with the stomach and intestines the respective responsibility of Duamutef and Qebehsenuef. The jars were often placed in wooden or stone chests that were similar in form to the rectangular coffins of this period. This style of canopic equipment continued through the Second Intermediate Period, with the only significant change being first the black colour of the box, followed by it being white, and a curving lid that recalled the roof of a naos. The boxes were also sometimes decorated with images of Anubis, each showing a different incarnation of that god.

A significant change occurs in the canopic equipment during the New Kingdom. Each of the jars begins to take on the relevant head of a Son of Horus (Hapy's jar acquired the head of an ape, Duamutef that of a canid, Qebehsenuef that of a falcon, and Imseti remains human), and the canopic chests are protected by images of the associated goddesses: Isis, Nepthys, Neith and Selqet. There are also some examples of miniature mummiform coffins being provided for each visceral bundle, perhaps an extension of the earlier cartonnage mask. By the end of the Twentieth Dynasty the canopic equipment was no longer placed near the feet but was sometimes divided up and placed on either side of the mummy.

As the viscera were returned to the body in the Twenty-first and Twenty-second Dynasties, the empty canopic equipment, when included in the tomb, was for show only and only evoked the invisible viscera. Some canopic jars were merely dummy jars, incapable of holding anything.

In the Late Period visceral bundles were once more placed in the jars. An additional feature of these jars appears in the inscriptions that punned on the names of the protective deities. By the Ptolemaic and Roman periods the use of canopic jars had died out and they, and the last, very small canopic chests, cease to form part of the burial equipment late in the Ptolemaic Period.

Shabtis

As the Afterlife was meant to be more perfect than life on earth, the Egyptians believed that it should be one of leisure and that no physical labour should be required after death. Thus, their tombs are filled with magical ways in which to improve the quality of life in the Hereafter. One such magical labour-saving device was the servant or serving statue, which developed into the *shabti*, also called *shawabti* and *ushebti*.

Servant statues are common in the Fifth and Sixth Dynasties and show people engaged in grinding grain, baking bread, making pottery, sieving beer, etc. These statues were thought to be magically animated in the Afterlife so that they could perform these services for the deceased, much as the images on the tomb walls (Chapter 6) were magically animated to carry out the activities that were depicted. The Old Kingdom images are not always servants but are identified as family members of the deceased, carrying out these mundane tasks for loved ones. In the Middle Kingdom these servant statues have developed into tomb models, wooden models illustrating daily-life activities. These too became magically alive and provided for the tomb-owner. However, these images were clearly providing services for the tomb-owner that would have been carried out by servants during the tomb-owner's lifetime. *Shabtis* carry out tasks that would have been assigned to the tomb-owner in the Afterlife as part of his service to the gods as well as providing for himself.

Shabtis first appear in the early Middle Kingdom, and only peter out during the Ptolemaic Period. They take the form of mummiform figures and are made out of a variety of materials: wood, glass, clay, wax, stone, bronze and, most commonly, faience. They can be of a variety of sizes and qualities; some are only a few centimetres in height, while others measure about half a metre, and the craftsmanship varies from exquisitely carved detailed statues to crude lumps of clay or mere wooden pegs. Each image was initially provided with its own coffin. Later, by the reign of Amenhotep II, they were placed in vertical shrine-shaped boxes, which, by the Nineteenth Dynasty, accommodated several hundred of these images, instead of the two *shabtis* that had been the norm until Amenhotep II's reign. *Shabtis* were a very important part of funerary equipment as can be seen by their ubiquitousness through time and presence in tombs of all social classes. *Shabtis* were made not only for humans as some sacred animals were also provided with these images: some Apis bulls have standard mummiform *shabtis* with bull-heads.

The purpose of the *shabtis* does not remain static through Egyptian history. Initially, they took over the role of the deceased's servants when they supplanted the tomb models. However, the *shabtis* could also act as the deceased himself (notice the parallel of *shabtis* being provided with coffins, like the mummy). As such, *shabtis* provided an alternative to *ka*-statues.

However, the most important role that the *shabti* played was to carry out any labour required of the deceased by the gods in the Afterlife. The gods would require the dead to cultivate the fields and engage in agricultural work, the mainstay of the Egyptian economy. Instead of the deceased having to do this, a substitute, the *shabti*, would carry out the necessary manual labour, allowing the deceased to enjoy a relaxed Afterlife.

Shabtis were animated by a magical spell, which first appeared in Dynasty XII, as Spell 472 of the Coffin Texts, and then as Chapter 6 in the Book of the Dead. The spells vary somewhat, but the gist of them is:

> O *shabti*, if [the deceased] is commanded to do any work in the realm of the dead: to prepare the fields, to irrigate the land or to convey sand from east to west; "Here I am" you shall say.

Aside from the spells, *shabtis* were generally inscribed with the name and title of the owner, and the soubriquet "the illuminated one", the Osiris, referring to the transformed status of the deceased in the Hereafter.

By the New Kingdom, *shabtis* were equipped with agricultural tools: model hoes and baskets. From model items, these implements were soon painted or carved directly onto the *shabti* itself. The number of *shabtis* also increased in the New Kingdom, and some tombs contain 365 figures, one for every day of the year, with thirty-six overseers, one overseer for each team of ten workers, making a total of 401 *shabtis* in a set. This number was often exceeded: Seti I owned about 700 *shabtis*, and Late Period burials were also known to contain several hundred. The term *shawabti* appears on images in the Seventeenth and Nineteenth Dynasties. The difference between it and the term *shabti* is unclear. Both words might derive from the word for stick or the word for food: both are feasible as the statuettes were often carved from wood and laboured to produce food. In the New Kingdom these images were commonly referred to as slaves, as is shown by receipts for these items.

Tutankhamun's calcite canopic box is shaped like a shrine with a sloping lid and protected by solar images and the four protective goddesses. The hieroglyphs are coloured blue–green, an allusion to Osiris. Cairo Museum, photograph by M. A. Muhammed.

In the Third Intermediate Period *shabtis* were being mass produced and became quite crude, as well as plentiful, a trend that
carried on into the Late Period. Their nature changed somewhat,
as is seen by the new term used to refer to them: *ushabti*. This
means "to answer" and clearly refers to the fact that, when the
gods raised the call to work, the image would answer and say
"here I am".

Provisioning the tomb

Tombs were equipped with many objects necessary for the well-
being of the deceased. The most crucial of these were the trap-
pings surrounding the body. However, a well-appointed tomb
had to include other features to ensure the continuous comfort of
the deceased in the Hereafter. These items ranged from the basic

food supply that would provide eternal nourishment for the deceased to clothing, furniture, games, and other objects that would make life permanently pleasant in the Fields of Iaru. All these three-dimensional objects augmented the two-dimensional illustrations on the tomb walls, as well as the tomb-models mentioned above that also magically served the dead in the Afterlife (Chapter 6). There is some debate as to whether objects were specifically manufactured for the tomb or whether the tomb-owner was buried with the belongings that had served him in life; the answer seems to be a combination of the two.

Food offerings

Food offerings were the focal point for the cult of the dead. Just as food was vital for life on this earth, it was considered crucial for continued survival, and great pains were taken to adequately provide for the deceased in the Afterlife from the earliest times onward. The offering lists that featured prominently in tombs mainly list food-stuffs.

A funerary meal from a Second Dynasty princess's tomb at Saqqara included such delicacies as quail, barley porridge, pigeon stew, grilled fish, a joint of beef and beef ribs, kidneys, bread, wine, fruit and cheese, and cake for dessert. It is ironic that the lady, had she been alive, would have been unable to enjoy much of this feast as one side of her lower jaw was inoperational owing to an injury or disease that she had sustained early in life. It is hoped that in her renewed and perfect state she could have enjoyed these delicacies so thoughtfully provided.

Tombs of the Old and Middle Kingdoms were provided with hollow limestone and calcite boxes carved in the shape of joints of meat or poultry that once contained these food offerings. In the Middle Kingdom these offerings were augmented with large pottery jars half-filled with a mud platform, containing mummified meat offerings (see Chapter 4), similar to the ones found in the

Tutankhamun's tomb was filled with things ranging from ritual items such as funerary beds and images of divinities to everyday objects such as chairs, beds, clothes, weapons and food-stuffs. Cairo Museum, photograph by Lehnert and Landrock.

stone boxes. By the New Kingdom these stone boxes were replaced by wooden coffinets whose shapes mirrored their contents. Tutankhamun had over forty such victual mummies to ensure that he would be well fed in the Hereafter.

Jars, plates and baskets filled with different types of bread, both sweet and savoury, have also been found in Egyptian tombs. The high percentage of sand in many of these loaves has led scholars to suggest that they were produced specially for funerals and that loaves consumed in daily life would be made of finer flour; this is still debated.

Fruits and vegetables are also found as part of the funerary food provisions, together with honey, oils and a variety of beverages, with wine and beer being the most prevalent. Although beer was the national drink, Tutankhamun did not seem to be fond of it as his tomb is provisioned only with wine jars.

Objects of daily life

The few relatively intact tombs that have been discovered were filled with an astonishing array of objects used by the deceased in his daily life, with some of these being specifically produced for the tomb, or house of eternity. Clothing, folded and stored in wooden chests, provides an insight into Egyptian fashion. It appears that some clothes, used when the person was a child, were preserved and interred with the body, as was the case with Tutankhamun. Perhaps there is an element of the belief that when one is reborn, one will need the same size of clothes as were used in one's childhood on earth.

Cosmetics and toilette sets are also included in tombs. Mirrors, a part of the toilette set, played a dual role in the tomb: they were useful objects, as well as being metaphors for life after death. Similarly, some of the cosmetic containers carved in the shape of lotuses also evoked the eternal existence. Some of the cosmetic jars, notably those for costly oils, are actually not fully hollowed out, so only a little of these precious substances were actually offered, although the appearance of the exterior of the jar contradicted this.

The majority of the furniture that has been found in tombs appears to have been used during people's lifetimes. Tutankhamun's furniture shows how he grew, as chairs from his infancy to adulthood are included in his tomb. However, the funerary beds found in his tomb probably served a ritual purpose. These enormous gilded couches with lion, hippopotamus or cow heads (each couch had only one type of animal) are not usable and are three-dimensional representations of some of the funerary beds shown on coffins and funerary texts and in tombs. The use of this ritual furniture, probably reserved for royal burials, is unclear, although it is likely to have been associated with the regenerative process.

Games, weapons and chariots have also been found in tombs. On one level these were all provided so that the deceased could amuse

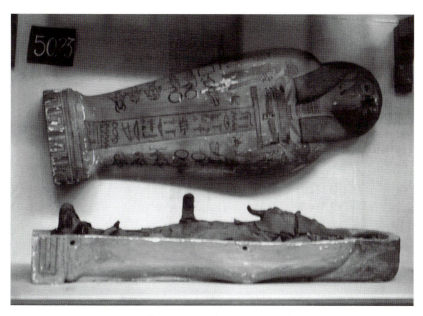

An Osiris "Corn Mummy" that is shaped as Osiris with an erection, and is stuffed with grain. Both the stuffing and the pose are symbolic of resurrection and fertility. Cairo Museum.

himself in the Afterlife. However, another level of interpretation would suggest that the objects used for hunting were indicative of the deceased's commitment to *maat*. Hunting, in Egyptian iconography, is often a way of showing control over disorder and chaos: humans tame chaotic nature and thus establish *maat*, and the inclusion in a tomb of the tools of hunting, together with representations of the sport on the tomb's walls, would establish *maat* in the eternal life of the tomb-owner. Similarly, certain games, such as the board game *Senet* (similar perhaps to Parchesi or Ludo), were a metaphor for the various trials and challenges that the deceased would have had to endure on his way through the Underworld to eternity.

Thus, the objects that filled the tomb provided for every comfort in the deceased's Afterlife, as well as playing a symbolic role in the deceased's transformation from a mummy to an eternal *akh*.

Corn Mummies and Osiris Beds

Two curious genres of objects found in tombs that have a purely symbolic/religious function are Osiris Beds and Corn Mummies. The former consist of a shallow wooden outline figure of Osiris, crowned with the *atef* crown, clasping the crook and the flail in his hands, and facing right. The figure is filled with earth and planted with grain that had just started to germinate before being put into the tomb. These cereal beds, symbolizing growth, fertility and rebirth, are known from the New Kingdom, although earlier examples in the shape of rectangles, rather than Osiris, are known from the Middle Kingdom. These Osirid cereal beds were possibly inspired by Coffin Text 269: Becoming Barley of Lower Egypt. In Chapter 269 the deceased is identified with this plant growing on the ribs of Osiris, who nourishes it and the deceased. These Osiris Beds were probably the precursors of the Corn Mummies.

Osiris Corn Mummies are a type of artifact peculiar to the later periods of Egyptian history. They consist of mummiform objects, about thirty-five to fifty centimetres in length, wrapped in linen bandages and placed in falcon-headed coffins. The mummies themselves are wrapped in the shape of a miniature figure of an ithyphallic Osiris and contain a mixture of grain and clay–sand which reflects the idea of sprouting cereals, the potential of the black soil and rebirth. Many of these had a wax mask that was painted green, with facial features highlighted in gold leaf. Texts on the falcon-headed coffin linked these images to Ptah-Sokar-Osiris, the popular funerary deity of Egypt's later periods. Variations of these Corn Mummies take the form of clay Osiris figures that are wrapped in linen bandages and placed on a linen bed, stuffed with grains of barley. The whole ensemble is enclosed in rush matting.

Barley (*it* in Egyptian) and emmer wheat (*bdt* in Egyptian) were fundamental to the Egyptian diet, providing the basis for bread and beer. Thus, these cereal mummies represent not only Osiris and the possibilities of rebirth, regeneration and resurrection that he represented but the actual grains and green shoots that were manifestations of that rebirth, and the source of the food that sustained life.

Notes

[1] Throughout Egyptian history the convention for the wealthy was to show men as red from being bronzed in the sun and women to be a yellowy-cream, showing that they remained inside and did not have to venture out without a sunshade. During the Amarna period this changed, and images of women were often painted the same reddish brown as men. This change in coloration was short-lived; artists reverted to the conventional shades for the sexes shortly after the end of the period.

6
The tomb

That the tomb provided one with an eternal cosmos is evident from its name: the House for Eternity. Building a tomb was almost as important as constructing a house or having a family, as the "house of death is for life", according to Prince Hardjedef (Dynasty IV, the son of King Khufu, builder of the Great Pyramid). Tombs, being eternal, were built of imperishable materials whenever possible, after the early Old Kingdom. Houses, used only during the course of a transitory lifetime, were made of mud brick and other perishable materials. Tombs were divided into two portions: the offering place or decorated tomb-chapel, where the cult for the deceased was celebrated, located above ground, and the burial chamber, where the body was interred, located below ground. In Egyptian the former was known as *huwt aat* or *shepes* and the latter as *khenet*. The underground chamber was the equivalent of the underworld, the realm of Osiris, the shaft or passage leading from the surface – often within or close to the tomb-chapel – being a liminal area of transition, perhaps akin to the passage to the underworld. The tomb chapel was in the land of the living, where the *ka* and *ba* could interface with the living, and was associated with solar imagery. Thus, the deceased was associated with both the sun god Ra as well as with Osiris, both divinities involved with rebirth, resurrection and eternal life.

The portion of the tomb accessible to most visitors today, and certainly in the past, is the tomb-chapel or superstructure, which is frequently the only decorated portion of the tomb. The burial chamber, or substructure, was rarely decorated, and its walls were frequently left unfinished. Texts suggest that the ancient Egyptians vied with one another to have beautifully decorated tombs in order to attract not only their own family members but also passers-by who came to visit the tombs of their own relatives, or to examine their own tombs that were under construction (see below). Visitors would thus speak the name of the deceased, and perhaps recite an offering formula to them (Chapter 7), so that their spirit would flourish in the Afterworld.

Location

Whenever possible cemeteries were located on the west side of the Nile, opposite the corresponding settlement on the east. This corresponds to the metaphor of human life as parallel to the path of

the sun: rising in the east and setting (dying) in the west. However, the Egyptians were pragmatic people, and if, as in parts of Middle Egypt, the west bank had a wider floodplain more suitable for agriculture, and sandy desert less suited for tomb construction, the east would be chosen for burial (the crossing of the river also played a role parallel to the sun's journey on the solar boat through the sky). In some instances, perhaps in the later periods of Egyptian history when cemeteries were crowded, settlements located on the west bank (such as Athribis in Middle Egypt) would situate their tombs further west of the town. This reversal of normal orientations could lead to some modifications in the arrangement of the tomb-chapels, in order to ensure that the actual offering place remained facing west.

Tombs were generally located away from settlements for two reasons. The first was purely pragmatic in terms of the practical exploitation of land and materials, matters of hygiene, and safety from carrion-eating animals. The second was more religious; a distance from a cemetery was thought to deter the meddling of restless or mischievous spirits in human affairs.

The location of a tomb within a cemetery was also significant, although this was more an indication of the deceased's economic and social status, rather than a religious statement. In royal necropoleis, proximity to the pharaoh increased the importance of one's tomb and allowed the tomb-owner to benefit from the pharaoh's reflected divinity. Especially in the Old Kingdom, a tomb plot might be a gift from the king, a very tangible mark of royal favour. In non-royal cemeteries, especially in Upper Egypt, where we have a more complete record of funerary remains than from Lower Egypt, the location of one's tomb along the cliffs was indicative of status. At Beni Hasan the most important people, the nomarchs or governors, had tombs located in the highest level of the cliff, where the best quality rock was located. Individuals of lesser importance and wealth had either much smaller tombs in the same level or simpler shaft tombs lower down on the slope. The lower on the slope was one's tomb, the lower one's rank,

A funerary papyrus showing Osiris sitting in judgement with the deceaseds, who have successfully weighed their hearts against the feather of maat, before him. Cairo Museum.

The rock tombs of Meir are cut into the cliffs, some with elaborate doorways, although most are relatively modest. Meir.

until the poorest graves were located at the desert edge and consisted of shallow pits dug into the desert gravel, similar in style to tombs of the Predynastic period. Of course, if a cemetery was used over time, then later tombs would squeeze in wherever they could find space, and considerations of rank and status would become secondary. Quality of rock could also reverse this hierarchy. At Thebes, the best rock lies in the lower part of the cliffs and valley floor, so those wishing to carve the decoration of their chapel had to forego a prominent site in favour of one sunk below ground surface.

The placement of cemeteries, especially royal cemeteries, was often dictated by religious considerations. The earliest royal burial place of Abydos was probably chosen because of its identification as the gateway to the Underworld. Its later association with Osiris further sanctified it and made it a focal point for funerary rituals. The pyramids of the Old Kingdom, solar symbols promising the rebirth and resurrection of the kings, were probably positioned with regard to the main sun temple of Egypt, located at Heliopolis. The Valley of the Kings was chosen for the burials of New Kingdom royalty owing to the pyramidal peak that dominates the sky above the *wadi* (valley), as well as for its inaccessibility.

Tomb construction

Tombs are of two major types, rock cut and free-standing, although there are plenty that span the divide. The former are most common in Upper Egypt, while the latter are more the norm in Lower Egypt. This division is mainly due to the topography of the two regions, as well as the availability of raw materials. Furthermore, in areas lacking secure bedrock, tomb chambers could be erected in shallow cuttings in the soil or gravel; such rooms could be of masonry or mud brick, sometimes with a vaulted roof. A superstructure might then be erected on the levelled ground surface above.

Rock-cut tombs are simply carved into the cliff face, or down into the bedrock (in which case they are more commonly called "shaft tombs"). An initial narrow exploratory tunnel was carved horizontally into the cliff in order to judge the quality of the rock. Tools such as wood and stone pounders/hammers, and chisels made of a copper–bronze alloy, annealed for strength, were the basic implements used for these excavations. If the rock were stable, this tunnel would provide the central guideline for the carving of the tomb. The tomb would be laid out using simple measuring tools such as cubit measures and long pieces of string, marked with length measurements at appropriate intervals. Markings in red ink that result from these guidelines are still visible on the ceilings and walls of many tombs. Once the tomb was cut, using the middle of the central passage as the guiding point, the walls were smoothed and prepared for decoration, where appropriate. Generally, only the chapel was decorated, although there are exceptions where the burial chamber is decorated. The shaft or sloping passage that led

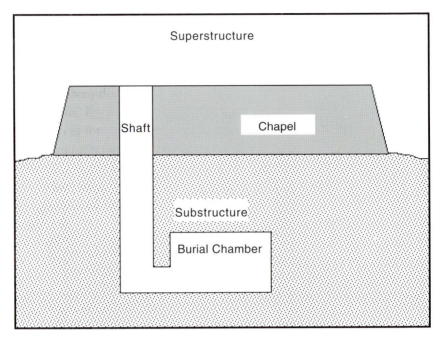

The superstructures of mastabas were the focal point of the cult of the deceased and the main area of decoration, while the substructures contained the burials and were sealed after the interment. Drawing by John Swanson.

to the burial chamber that was sealed after the burial would usually be reached from the floor of the tomb-chapel or be accessed from the area directly outside the tomb's entrance.

Free-standing tombs were constructed out of brick or stone,[1] and were, until the New Kingdom, usually built in the shape of *mastabas* (Arabic for bench; the term was used by early excavators because of their resemblance to the benches that form part of modern vernacular architecture). From the New Kingdom on, small temples or other divine sanctuaries provided the model for free-standing tombs, although *mastabas* were still used at some sites. The plans of these built tombs differ from the rock-cut counterparts because they could be more flexible as they did not require quarrying through solid rock. Decoration was carved into the limestone slabs that lined the chapel, which with *mastabas*

The necropolis of Beni Hasan shows social stratification with the most important and wealthy individuals buried in the highest levels of the cliff in elaborate rock-cut tombs, with people of lesser importance interred in simpler tombs in the same level. Lower down, poorer and less significant individuals were buried in shaft tombs whose superstructures consisted of small mud brick chapels or offering emplacements. The poorest interments would have been dug into the desert margins.

could be either against the east face or inside the structure of the mastaba itself. The burial-chambers of these tombs would be cut into the bedrock, or built in shallow cuttings below the tomb where local conditions demanded it. The location of the tomb entrance shows considerable variability. Many Old Kingdom sepulchres have shafts that began in the roof of the *mastaba*. Some Old Kingdom tombs at Bubastis, in the Delta, consist of stone-built chambers accessed by stone-lined shafts that were set into the wet delta soil.

The builders

Tombs were constructed by specialized artisans, although non-specialists were employed to carry out the moving of heavy blocks and some of the purely physical labour of levelling and general preparation of a site. The artisans in charge of construction were divided into gangs or teams, with names such as (in the Old Kingdom) Friends of Khufu, or Drunkards of Menkaure. These teams worked in shifts and lived near the site. Some workmen's villages have been excavated at Giza, Lahun, and Deir el-Medina. The people involved in the construction of royal tombs would be paid by the king or the state, while those who worked on non-royal tombs (and may often have been "borrowed" from the royal teams) would be paid by individuals.

The workers' cemetery at Giza is particularly interesting in providing evidence of work-related accidents. Some of the mummified remains show that various limbs had broken and been set during the course of pyramid construction, while one man had dropped a heavy rock on his toe, crushing it. Clearly, a medical unit must have been in residence at the site during construction.

Techniques of tomb decoration

Much of the current information concerning the logistics of tomb decoration comes from the New Kingdom tombs in the Valley of the Kings, and from Deir el-Medina, the village of the workmen who constructed the royal tombs. Physical evidence from unfinished or partially completed tombs may be combined with textual sources in the form of ostraka with lists of workmen, their work schedules, amounts they were paid, and records of the tools they were given, to provide details concerning the organization and execution of tomb construction during this period.

Simply put, once a section of the tomb had been prepared for adornment by two teams of workmen, one for each side of the tomb, work began on its decoration. If a wide chamber was being constructed, the two end walls would usually be freed from the matrix first, thus delineating the extent of the room. Thus, the end walls might be decorated in advance of the preceding side walls, thus reversing the expected order. A layer of plaster would

The tomb of Horemheb is unfinished, and thus the various states of tomb decoration are clearly illustrated, starting from the grid, the drawings and corrections, to the initial carving of the rock. Valley of the Kings 57.

usually be laid on the rock wall prior to decoration. If the rock was of good quality, only a thin wash would be used; if not so good, thick mud plaster and a substantial layer of gypsum could be added.

A grid was usually laid out to provide the basis for a rough sketch in red ink of the text and decorations that were to be carved and/or painted onto the wall. The chief draftsman would correct the sketch in black, and then, if the tomb were to be only painted, the artists would set to work. If the tomb were to be carved and then painted, the carving away of the background stone, leaving the *bas* (low) relief in place, would be the next step. The master carver would make corrections prior to the final part of the decoration: the painting of the relief. Paints were made of natural materials, generally ochres quarried in the desert, or ground-up malachite and copper for greens and blues. In some instances the tomb-owner died while the tomb was being constructed, so that

The Early Dynastic enclosure at the Shunet ez-Zebib where the cult of the deceased king, Khasekhemwy, was celebrated. Abydos.

The Step Pyramid was built by the architect Imhotep who was later deified. This complex included not only the pyramid and mortuary temple, but a series of other dummy-buildings that were associated with rituals for divine kingship. Saqqara.

the carved decoration is abandoned and the tomb is hastily finished in paint. There are some examples where the tomb-owner died and the workmen simply laid down their tools and left the tomb unfinished. This method of decoration was employed regardless of whether the tomb was rock-cut or free standing.

Generally, the exterior of tombs was carved in sunk relief so that when the sun hit the decoration it would still be visible. In sunk relief the details are incised into the stone. The interior of tombs tended to be carved in *bas* (low) relief, enhanced by paint. This could be easily seen in the dim interior of the tomb-chapel and would not be destroyed by wind and sand abrasion, as it would if it were outside. The decoration of the burial chambers, when it occurred, was generally executed in paint. The shaft leading to the burial chamber was always left undecorated as it was a liminal area, balanced between the two worlds.

The artists

The artists who decorated royal tombs came from a specific royal workshop. In addition to working on the king's funerary monument, they might rent out their services to anyone who could afford their work. For most non-royal tombs throughout the Nile Valley, the artists came from different ateliers or workshops. As with the most ancient artists, not much is known about individual painters, save for a few, the majority of whom lived at Deir el-Medina in the New Kingdom. However, careful studies of tomb decoration have shown that the hands of certain artists can be recognized stylistically. The artist, or group of artists, who decorated the tomb of Queen Nefertari (QV 66) also had a hand in decorating the tomb of her father-in-law, Seti I (KV 17) and her sons and step-sons (KV 5).

It is unclear how certain ateliers were chosen. It is possible that specific ateliers were patronized by the king and thus gained popularity with the nobility. Alternatively, certain cemeteries, or areas of the necropoleis, might have been under the remit of a particular atelier. It is also possible that a group of workshops functioned in an area, and potential tomb-owners would choose one depending on prices, convenience and what was thought to be in vogue at the time. As with the artists, the work of certain ateliers can be recognized in terms of styles of painting/carving, as well as scene type. Clusters of tombs that are very similar in style are often found in cemeteries from all periods of Egyptian history. The Teti cemetery (Dynasty VI) at Saqqara is a good example of this, where an unusual hunting scene showing hunting dogs ripping an animal to shreds appears in more than one tomb.

Financing the tomb

Royal tombs were financed by the state. Certainly in the Old Kingdom when kings were buried in pyramids, the major unskilled element of the workforce was supplied by corvée labour: instead of paying taxes, peasants would work on the pyramid. This would generally be done during the four months of the annual inundation when the lands would lie fallow, although a regular workforce was employed all year round, until the completion of the monument. Thus, pyramid construction provided not only the king with a tomb, but the temporarily unemployed peasants with paid (food, clothing, shelter) work, the chance to avoid taxation and an act of piety by contributing to the construction of the house of eternity for the divine ruler, and thus contributing to the survival of the eternal cosmos. In the New Kingdom royal tombs continued to be financed by the state, but, because of the greater secrecy involved with the Valley of the Kings, and the more specialized construction methods used in the Mortuary Temples (see below), the excavation and construction of tombs was essentially left to specialists.

Generally, by the end of the Fourth Dynasty, non-royal individuals were responsible for financing their own tombs, although in some instances the king would provide land, stone, a part of the tomb or labourers (as was the case for the tomb of Debehen at Giza). At Giza, Khufu laid out streets of standard "nucleus" *mastabas* that were then allocated to individual members of the court for completion and decoration in accordance with their own tastes, but this seems to have been a unique initiative. Sometimes the parents or other family members of the deceased would provide certain elements of the burial: Queen Hetepheres II (Dynasty IV) provided her daughter Meresankh III with a granite sarcophagus. Several tombs contain texts that assert that the tomb-owner paid for the construction and decoration of the tomb. An inscription in the Sixth Dynasty *mastaba* of Remenuka (Giza, Central Field) states that he paid the artisans with bread, beer and linen. In the recently discovered tomb in Giza's Western Cemetery, Kai asserts how he himself paid for the construction of his tomb at Giza. Certainly, from the Middle Kingdom onward it was more usual for the tomb-owner and his family to be responsible for the construction and decoration of the tomb, with the king being less and less involved.

It is possible that, especially in provincial cemeteries, the local government or some other municipal body carved simple shaft tombs and sold them to potential tomb-owners. This is very similar to the modern tradition of purchasing cemetery plots. It has also been suggested by some scholars that even in royal cemeteries the option of "purchasing" a *mastaba* was offered, probably to help finance the construction of the royal burial place.

The evolution of tomb types

Royal tombs evolved separately from their non-royal counterparts, although the basis of the two types was the same, and various areas of parallelism are to be seen. The earliest tombs were shallow graves dug into the desert sand and gravel, marked with a pile of stone and sand, forming a *tumulus* (plural *tumuli*). Initially there seems to have been little apparent differentiation in the architecture or layout between noble and common graves, although the amount and quality of funerary equipment came to reflect social diversity. Later on, however, it is thought that the size of the grave and the tumulus depended, to some degree, on the importance of the individual. During the Naqada II period, some substructures became more complex, with the burial chambers being lined with brick, and, depending on the status and wealth of the deceased, divided into sections for the different grave goods. There is also one known example of a decorated tomb coming from this period, Tomb 100 at Hierakonpolis. This large tomb, probably belonging to a high-ranking individual, if not a local ruler, was mud-plastered and painted with scenes of fighting, hunting and river travel.

Royal tombs

By the Naqada III/Dynasty 0 period, royal tombs were clearly differentiated from non-royal burials. The majority of royal tombs of this and the Archaic period are located at the sacred site of Abydos, in the area now known as Umm el-Qaab (meaning mother of pots, owing to the density of pottery scatter on the desert surface); the exception were some kings of the early Second Dynasty, who were buried at Saqqara.

The subterranean many-chambered burial area of these tombs was constructed of mud brick sunk in the desert gravel at Abydos – or cut into the bedrock at Saqqara, with reed mats and wood lining some of the walls. The grave was covered by a gravel mound below the surface, and possibly one at ground level. The mounds, derived from the tumulus, represented the primeval mound that rose out of the primordial waters, and was the dwelling place of the creator-god and thus the route for the pharaoh's rebirth. This modest superstructure, possibly without a visible element, was accompanied by a pair of stone stelae inscribed with the king's name, identifying the owner of the edifice and marking out an offering place. Tombs of the king's servants were laid out in orderly rows around the royal burial. In the First Dynasty it seems that the servants either volunteered to die or were forcibly put to death so that they could accompany the king to the Afterworld. This practice had died out before the Old Kingdom, and statues are thought to have been substituted for these burials.

Large mud-brick enclosures, whose walls were decorated with the palace façade niching, were built over a kilometre away from the Abydos tombs, close to the cultivation, and were probably initially the principal focus of the mortuary cult of the king, while the associated mound tombs located in the desert were rarely visited. Similar enclosures were provided for the kings buried at Saqqara, but formed for the first time of stone.

The Third Dynasty saw a radical shift in royal burial practice with the construction of the step pyramid of King Djoser (Netjerikhet) at Saqqara. This burial complex was revolutionary as it was the first one to be built entirely of stone masonry. The complex combines the previously separate enclosure and tomb in one place, as well as adding to them. To some extent, this complex translates into stone the mud-brick, reed and wooden monuments that been its predecessors. The pyramid started as a giant stone *mastaba* that expanded, ultimately gaining in both height and width. Today the Step Pyramid consists of six steps that can be interpreted as a stairway to heaven (alluded to in the Pyramid Texts) and a subterranean burial chamber with connecting chambers and magazines that contained funerary goods. The rest of the complex consists of a symbolic Southern Tomb or cenotaph – a constant feature of royal tombs until the Middle Kingdom – a funerary temple to the north and the *heb-sed* courts, where the king's powers could be rejuvenated for eternity.

A significant change in royal funerary beliefs, and thus tomb design, occurred toward the end of the Third Dynasty. The Mortuary Temple had been located on the northern side of the pyramid. This must have been due to the belief that the king became one with the stars when he became an *akh*, and thus the temple was oriented to the most significant star, the North Star. By the reign of Snefru, at the start of the Fourth Dynasty, the

Dahshur was the site of many pyramids; the Bent Pyramid of Snefru (Dynasty IV) was a crucial step in the evolution of pyramids. The Black Pyramid of Amenemhat III (Dynasty XII) shows the degeneration of pyramid construction in the Middle Kingdom: it was made of mud brick with enforcing walls, but so ill-constructed that the roof of the burial chamber cracked even before the king's death. The king never used this pyramid, but one in Hawara; one of his wives was buried here. Dahshur.

Mortuary Temple had moved to the east, with an emphasis on solar orientation. The earlier stellar orientation was still important, but had paled in significance in comparison to the solar.

The "true" pyramid form evolved subsequently, with the first large-scale true pyramid being the North (Red, from the colour of the limestone used in its construction) Pyramid at Dahshur, built for Snefru in the Fourth Dynasty. The most famous examples remain, of course, the pyramids at Giza. The "true" pyramid was used by royalty until the end of the Second Intermediate Period, with a few exceptions. The complex that surrounded true pyramids differed entirely from earlier examples. The enormous rectangular enclosures of the Archaic period, and the Step Pyramid, were replaced by a completely new scheme. On the edge of the desert, perhaps linked to the Nile by a canal, lay a Valley Temple. A covered causeway connected it to the Mortuary Temple located on the east (rebirth) side of the pyramid. The enclosure wall now simply enclosed the pyramid, boat-pits[2] containing boats or alluding to the solar barque that the sun god and the dead pharaoh would use to cross the sky, and a subsidiary pyramid or cenotaph. Prior to the Twelfth Dynasty, pyramids were usually entered from the north. The burial chamber usually lay at, or below, ground level, under the centre of the pyramid. The cult of the king would be celebrated in the Valley and Mortuary Temples.

The straight sides of the "true" pyramids seem to have provided the king with a ramp to heaven.[3] They were constructed of massive stone blocks, quarried nearby, that were dragged into place over ramps by thousands of workers. The finished pyramid was covered with gleaming white limestone blocks from the Tura quarry, on the opposite side of the Nile, and topped by a pyramidion that was covered with gold or electrum (a gold and silver alloy), which would reflect the sun's rays in an impressive and blinding flash of light that would be visible for miles. Some pyramids had their lower courses cased with red granite. This was an allusion to their solar nature. To some extent this altered the shape by creating a slight pedestal, which made the monument more closely resemble the hieroglyph for pyramid.

The decorated areas of the pyramid complex grew progressively until the walls of both temples and the causeway were adorned. The interiors of the pyramids were, with the exception of the Step Pyramid, undecorated until the end of the Fifth Dynasty, when the burial chamber was first decorated with the Pyramid Texts. The causeways were probably the first element in the pyramid complex to be extensively decorated and were inscribed with the king's name and titles, as well as scenes of daily life, such as market scenes, archery events and different vignettes showing the phases of constructing the pyramid complex.

The Valley of the Kings was the location for New Kingdom royal burials. The natural pyramidal shape of the mountain and its inaccessibility were probably responsible for its choice as the royal necropolis. The peak was sacred to the goddess Meret-Seger, mistress of silence. Valley of the Kings.

The royal tombs of the First Intermediate Period, apparently generally located in the Saqqara area – although a very large anomalous "pyramid" is known near Manfalut in Middle Egypt – are little known. The thread of development of the royal tomb may be picked up again with the Eleventh Dynasty tombs at Thebes, in particular that of King Mentuhotep II. This unusual structure combined the tomb and mortuary temple with cult areas dedicated to the gods Amun-Re and Montu-Re. The tomb consisted of a platform, approached by a ramp, which was surmounted by a small pyramid, *mastaba* or perhaps tumulus (it is now ruined) surrounded by a colonnade. The burial chamber was accessed by a sloping passage from the rear of the monument that led deep into the mountain at Deir el-Bahari. The Twelfth Dynasty pharaohs reverted to pyramid construction in the north, eventually moving the entryway from the north, and elaborating the substructure with false passageways, dead ends and massive stone portcullises in an effort to thwart thieves.

As in the Early Dynastic period, the Mortuary Temples and cult centres of New Kingdom royalty were far removed from their tombs in the interest of security and convenience. The Ramesseum, Mortuary Temple of Ramesses II, is on the frontier between the cultivation and the desert, the point of intersection for the living and the dead. It is oriented eastward to the rising sun and the green of the fertile floodplain. Thebes/Luxor, West Bank.

The Second Intermediate Period tombs of the Hyksos (Dynasty XV) have yet to be discovered, although it is possible that they either followed a Canaanite burial pattern with mud-brick tombs or combined elements of Egyptian and Canaanite burials. The rulers of the Seventeenth Dynasty in Thebes were buried in tombs marked by mud-brick pyramids and simple, but substantial, substructures; their cemetery, at Dra' Abul-Naga, has recently been rediscovered. The last pyramid built by an Egyptian king was erected at the beginning of Dynasty XVIII by Ahmose I. It lay at Abydos, with its substructure in the desert behind it; it is uncertain, however, whether it was his actual tomb or merely a cenotaph at the holy city of Osiris, god of the dead.

The burial places of the kings of the New Kingdom were carved into the cliffs in the Valley of the Kings at Thebes (near modern

Luxor). For the first time since the Archaic period, the Mortuary Temples were separated from the tombs and located at the margins of the desert adjacent to the cultivation. The temples were the site of cult activity which had a three-fold focus: the king, the god Amun, and the sun god Re. The separation of the Mortuary Temple from the tomb was in part due to reasons of security, and a certain Ineni, superintendent of king Thutmose I's building projects, is thought to have been responsible for this innovation and the situation of the royal necropolis in the Valley of the Kings. By this time the trend had shifted from grandiose tombs that were clearly visible, and easily robbed, to having secure tombs that provided safety for the body and the funerary goods of the pharaoh. The location of the temples in the liminal areas at the boundary between the desert and the cultivated land emphasized their function as a link between the spirit of the dead king in the Afterworld, and the king's role as divine intermediary for the living population.

In this period, both the Mortuary Temples and the tombs proper were decorated, although the decorative schemes differed significantly. The exterior portions of the temples featured scenes showing events from the life of the king: the departure and return of successful trade or tribute-collecting expeditions to exotic locations, the defeat of the enemies of Egypt or the recording of an unusual event in the king's reign. The interior contained scenes of the king and the gods. Generally, as with cult temples of this period, the king is shown offering to different divinities, and the divinities are shown giving the king eternal life and making his memory flourish for eternity. This general scheme reflects that found earlier in the temples and causeway of a pyramid complex. However, it is important to note that New Kingdom temples were not simply for the funerary cult but were also dedicated to Amun-re, King of the Gods, who occupied the main sanctuary of the temple. The king's cult was relegated to a smaller room to the left of the main axis.

Tombs of the early Eighteenth Dynasty were located in hidden places in the Valley, with no obvious markers. They consisted of passages cut into the rock, opening into pillared halls, and then turning abruptly and descending into the burial chamber. The burial chamber was the focus of decoration and was painted with portions from the Amduat (see Chapter 2), giving the illusion that a giant papyrus had been unrolled and stuck against the walls. The pillars in the pillared hall were also decorated with more traditional religious scenes, and in a more conventional style, depicting the pharaoh and a divinity embracing, the pharaoh being given life (with the *ankh* sign), or other scenes showing the close relationship between a deity and the deceased king. The architecture of the whole tomb could be seen as an attempt to represent the path through the Underworld, with the decorations of the burial chamber being the culmination of this passage, and with the triumphant resurrection of the deceased being the end result. Akhenaten's tomb was an anomaly, being located at Amarna, and not being constructed or decorated in the same way as other royal tombs. The decoration featured the Aten, as well as scenes from the life of the king, as opposed to the king with a variety of gods. Osiris, god of the dead, had also been strictly excluded from Akhenaten's new religion and is conspicuous by his absence in the royal tomb at Amarna.

Nineteenth and Twentieth Dynasty royal tombs differed from those of their predecessors in that they were generally carved in a straight line, down into the bedrock, which earned them the name syringe or syrinx (after the Greek flutes) tombs. There were occasional chambers going off the main corridor and the burial chamber, although this was not always the case. The decoration of these tombs was very different: generally the entire tomb was decorated, not just the burial chamber and pillared hall. The decoration consisted of properly painted scenes showing the dead king and various divinities as well as texts from several different religious books, some of which were illustrated, while others were not. The doorways of these tombs were well marked with decorated façades. Clearly (and fruitlessly), the pharaohs were trusting their security to police patrols and massive stone sarcophagi that

A Fourth Dynasty mastaba that illustrates the idea of tomb as house, with an outside wall, and a porticoed façade. Giza.

are difficult to breach. The Valley of the Kings was abandoned as a royal necropolis by the end of the Twentieth Dynasty.

The Twenty-first and Twenty-second Dynasty kings were buried in the Delta at Tanis. These tombs consisted of cult chapels (now destroyed) on the surface, with the actual burial located in a stone-built subterranean burial chamber. The royal tombs, together with the tombs of high-ranking individuals of the period, were built within the enclosure wall of the Amun temple, rather than in a separate royal necropolis. This practice of including tombs of important individuals within the temple precincts continued for successive dynasties, with the exception of Dynasty XXV, the Nubian Dynasty, whose pharaohs were buried in small pyramids with Mortuary Temples, in Nubia at el-Kurru and Nuri. The tombs of the Ptolemaic rulers have yet to be discovered, although the sepulchres of non-royal individuals of that time have been excavated at Alexandria and other sites throughout Egypt.

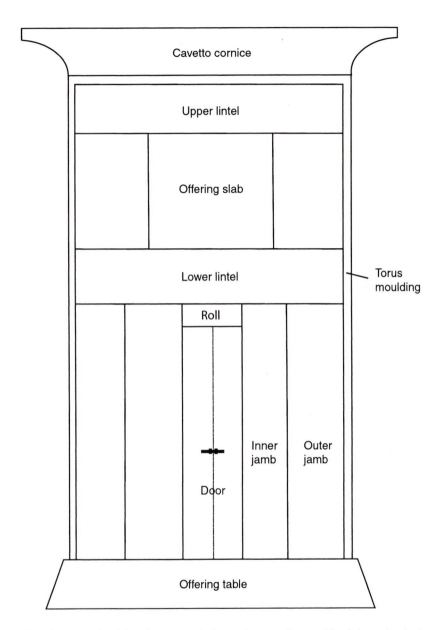

The elements of a false door varied, depending on the wealth of the individual and the complexity of the tomb, but the main components of an inscribed door and offering place were standard for most Egyptian tombs. Drawing by Violaine Chauvet.

Non-royal tombs

It was mainly after the unification of Egypt that extremely sharp distinctions were made between non-royal and royal burials beyond those of size, grave goods and decoration. Burials of non-royal individuals from the Early Dynastic period onward were of two types: free-standing tombs (either in *mastabas* that continued to be built throughout Egyptian history or in temple-like structures that came into vogue in the New Kingdom) and rock-cut tombs, which acted as the focus of the cult of the deceased, all having a simple shaft or stairway within or nearby leading to a burial chamber. These tomb types remained constant throughout most of Egypt's history, with minor variations.

The *mastabas* of the First and Second Dynasties were constructed of mud brick, and many were very literal interpretations of the concept of "tomb as house" to the extent of including toilets and lavatories in the structure of the tomb. Generally, a niche placed at either end of the eastern façade constituted the offering place.

After the Third Dynasty, mud- and stone-built *mastabas* became common for the cultic focus (Chapter 7), with burial chambers being reached either from the roof of the *mastaba* or from just outside. Unlike the mud-brick structures of the first two dynasties, the mud- and stone-built *mastabas* of the Third and early Fourth Dynasties were generally not organized as a house that one could walk through. Instead, on the eastern face, these solid structures contained one or two focal points for the celebration of the cult of the deceased. During the Third and Fourth Dynasties, the simple niches of the earlier dynasties were elaborated into chapels of various forms decorated with images of the deceased, offerings, offering lists, and some scenes of daily life.

Some chapels, from the mid-Fourth Dynasty onwards, became multi-room; thus one could walk through these *mastabas*. These chambers were decorated with scenes illustrating many varied aspects of daily life. The size and complexity of the tomb-chapel depended on the wealth and position of the tomb-owner. The burial chambers for these tomb-chapels were accessed either from the roof or from within the tomb-chapel proper, leading to the burial chamber carved from the bedrock below. The burial chambers were frequently positioned so as to lie beneath the false door or offering focus of the tomb. They remain plain until the end of the Fifth Dynasty, when a number of chambers are found adorned with lists and depictions of offerings. Interestingly, this coincides closely with the adoption of Pyramid Texts within royal pyramids.

The false door was one of the most important features of a tomb and was an integral element of any tomb, regardless of whether it was a rock-cut or free-standing edifice. This was where the majority of prayers and offerings to the deceased were made. As the name suggests, it is a door, but one that was not usable as it was made of solid stone. The false door was the point in the tomb where the *ka* as well as the *ba* could interface with living beings. It consisted of an elaborately carved entryway leading to the Afterworld: the top was surmounted by a cavetto cornice, and the entire door defined by a torus moulding. The upper lintel was separated from the lower lintel by an offering slab that showed the deceased in front of a table piled high with offerings of food and drink. Lines of text gave the tomb-owner's name and titles and listed the various delicacies provided for the Afterlife. The door itself appeared below the lower lintel. Both one- and two-flap doors locked by a bolt are shown as false doors. Carved in stone above the door was a rolled-up mat which in a real house could be let down to hide and shade the door and provide privacy if the door were left open. The door was flanked by inner and outer jambs which frequently bore inscriptions relating to the deceased's name and titles, as well as images of offering bearers, or family members. An offering table was located directly in front of the door, and this was where offerings were placed or poured. Although the false door was within the tomb, it was often carved in sunk relief, a style that was usually reserved for the exterior of

The slit allows Ti (Dynasty V) to look out of his serdab. The slit is flanked by carved images of priests incensing the image so that, magically, Ti's statue would be given revivifying incense to breathe and his ka would flourish eternally. Saqqara, photograph by J. Swanson.

buildings as it showed well in direct sunlight. The reason for this is that the door was exterior to the true interior of the tomb, the burial chamber, as well as being exterior to the Afterworld. Thus, the sunk relief was a nice conceit that shifted the boundaries of interior and exterior between the two worlds.

Another important architectural element in Old Kingdom tombs was the *serdab*. *Serdab* means cellar, tunnel or enclosed storage room in Arabic and accurately describes these chambers that contained statues of the deceased, as well as statues of workers grinding grain, sieving beer, making pottery or cooking. These model workers provided services for the deceased in the Afterlife and sometimes were inscribed with the names of the family members who had given the statues as offerings to the deceased. The statue of the deceased that was located in the *serdab* was sometimes pro-

The interior of rock-cut tombs varied. Some were single chambered and empty, while other single-chambered tombs were enlivened with pillars or columns which were sometimes structurally unnecessary but aesthetically pleasing or ritually significant. The pillars in this elaborate multi-chambered, painted rock-cut tomb are structurally important. Meir.

vided with a slit in the wall so that it could look out at the visitors who passed through the tomb and count the number and kinds of offerings and prayers made. This was especially easy as most *serdab*s were located near or opposite the false door. *Serdabs* rarely appear as part of tomb architecture outside the Old Kingdom. However, throughout Egyptian history tomb-chapels frequently contained statues of the deceased that were also a focal point of the funerary offering rituals and prayers.

Mastabas are generally superseded on "flat" sites by free-standing "temple–tomb" combinations from the end of the Eighteenth Dynasty onward. With some variations, they are found throughout Egypt. These consist of an enclosed courtyard fronted by a pylon. This leads to a cult-chapel consisting of one or more rooms. In the New Kingdom this is surmounted by a small pyramid, which is not found in later examples of this temple tomb

A Dynasty XIX pyramidal tomb-chapel where the cult of the deceased would be celebrated. Deir el-Medina.

type of the Ptolemaic period (e.g. the tomb of Petosiris at Tuna el-Gebel). The burial chamber is reached from a shaft in the courtyard or the chapel and may be a single room or a part of a major complex of chambers, shafts and galleries.

Rock-cut tombs are generally used where the local topography was unsuitable for *mastaba* or temple–tombs. They are particularly common in Upper Egypt and parts of Middle Egypt where the topography lent itself to such structures. The tomb-chapel was cut into the cliff face, and the burial chambers were reached via a shaft or sloping passage that was cut either inside or just outside the chapel. The basic architectural shape of these tombs was very similar throughout Egyptian history, with variations occurring as a result of the time period or stylistic preferences of certain areas. At some sites, additional elements were built onto the front of the rock-cut focus, and thus there are a number of examples of hybrids between the various tomb types – in certain cases of all three.

This Ptolemaic temple–tomb-chapel of Petosiris, dedicated to his father and brother, takes the shape of a rectangular Late Egyptian temple, as well as elements of domestic architecture (temples were also divine houses) in the form of a surrounding fence and a portico. It is decorated in a mixed Graeco-Egyptian style. Tuna el-Gebel.

Most rock-cut tombs consisted of one or more chambers that were cut straight back into the cliff face, their roofs often supported by pillars or columns. Sometimes, as with Middle Kingdom examples at Beni Hasan and New Kingdom examples at el-Amarna, the latter had elaborate capitals, such as lotus buds or papyrus umbels. Often, in tombs of the Middle and New Kingdoms, statues of the deceased were carved from the living rock in the last chamber of the tomb. This small chamber, together with the false door, was an important focal point for the celebration of the cult of the deceased. Theban tombs of the Eighteenth Dynasty generally took on a "T" shape, with the cross-bar running parallel to and just behind the cliff face. The focal point was at the base of the "T", deep in the rock, aligned

A scene of apiculture from the tomb of Pabasa (Dynasty XXVI) that was probably inspired by the tomb of Rekhmire (TT 100, Dynasty XVIII). Asasif, West Bank, Luxor.

with the tomb's doorway. Nineteenth Dynasty and later tomb-chapels continue with this distinctive shape but vary the tomb type by adding new elements or modifying existing ones. At Thebes, small pyramids were added to some tombs, either on a platform above the entrance or sometimes actually enclosing the chapel (see below).

Earlier New Kingdom tombs have simple substructures, but, from the middle of the Eighteenth Dynasty, elaborate examples appear, with passageways and pillared halls rivalling royal sepulchres. In Ramesside times, it became common practice for tombs to descend in a spiral. These rooms and corridors were generally undecorated, but a few imitated royal tombs in being decorated with the Amduat or similar works.

Tomb-chapels of the Twenty-first Dynasty are essentially unknown, most burials being made in simple shaft tombs, with undecorated burial chambers. A few Twenty-second Dynasty examples have a small chapel built on the surface directly above the shaft. It was not until the Twenty-fifth and Twenty-sixth Dynasties that monumental tomb-chapels reappear. Decoratively, they alluded to more archaic types of tombs, but evolved a unique architectural style. At Thebes, vast "funerary palaces" were built for highly placed nobles, partly built of brick, partly rock cut. Their chapels followed earlier decorative practice, while their burial corridors aped the style of Ramesside royal tombs. Versions of these tombs were also found at other sites. A unique Lower Egyptian style is found, with the superstructure limited to a square of niched mud-brick exterior walls, fitted with false doors and offering slabs. A huge shaft led to the small burial chamber. This was highly decorated with funerary texts and images and contained an anthropomorphic stone coffin, which was also decorated. In some instances, some of the underground chambers were also inscribed with autobiographical texts. The security of the burial was entrusted to an extensive, and elaborate, filling of sand, which was successful in the majority of excavated tombs of this type.

Late Period tombs take various forms. Late Period royal tombs seem to have followed Third Intermediate Period patterns, while private tombs include *mastabas* and temple–tombs, as well as more modest chapels, all with burial shafts below. Communal catacombs also start to appear

Graeco-Roman period sepulchres vary greatly, in part depending on whether the owners preferred Egyptian or Greek/Roman practices. In either case, communal arrangements were very common. Family tombs were built to act as mausolea that could be easily reopened to receive more bodies with ease. The bodies rested in narrow *loculi*, or horizontal niches, cut into the rock.

Although the ideal was always to have both a chapel and a burial place, many were unable to afford anything more than a simple shaft. Shaft tombs are among the simplest and most economical of tomb types. Although a stela or offering table might be placed at the top of a shaft, these tombs generally consist of shafts cut into the bedrock or desert gravel and open up into a chamber or a series of chambers. These tombs are known from the Old Kingdom onward and are used whenever there is solid gravel or rock. In some cases when there is no solid foundation, such as in many parts of the Delta, these shafts are dug into the ground and then lined with stone. For the most part this tomb type is undecorated.

Tomb decoration

The decorated part of a tomb that is visited is generally the tomb-chapel or superstructure. The substructure or burial chamber, which is sealed off, is sometimes decorated. The decoration of the superstructure and substructure differs significantly. Royal tombs had a different schema of decoration to that of non-royal tombs, although they shared basic conceptions: the superstructure had scenes rooted in the world of the living, the substructure that of the dead.

Accordingly, tomb-chapels (and in the case of royal tombs this role would be taken by the mortuary and/or valley temples), which were the focus of the cult of the deceased, were decorated with scenes of "daily life", with a strong focus on earthly activities. Thus, tomb-chapels are enlivened with scenes of leisure moments that the tomb-owner might have enjoyed in life, including hunting, fishing and feasting, as well as the production of objects necessary in this life and the next, such as furniture, clothing and jewellery. The most important scenes were those illustrating food production, with butchers, fishermen, farmers, vintners, brewers and bakers all shown at their tasks so that the tomb-owner would enjoy all the good things in life in the Hereafter.

It is important to remember that the Egyptians viewed their illustrations and inscriptions as magical. Once something was described, written, or said out loud (similar to the later Biblical equivalent of the power of the "thought" and the "word" that was conceived and spoken, thus creating the world), it became real. Thus, the paintings on the tomb walls would, presumably after certain rites had been celebrated in the tomb, become magically "active", and become real as they were needed. Thus, the depictions could provide for the tomb-owner in the Hereafter, even after the priests might have given up an active role in the cult (Chapter 7).

Royal offering places (chapels/temples) also showed scenes of earthly life. However, in addition to the usual scenes of food production, etc., they also showed the king's communion with his fellow deities. Thus royal tomb decoration included several scenes of the king as a god, as well as interacting with gods, and thus ensuring the blessing of the gods over the king and the land in this world and the next.

Although on one level tomb art showed scenes of daily life, these scenes can be read as metaphors or allegories. The tomb was a re-creation of the cosmos, and one of the major functions of tomb decoration was to show the establishment and maintenance of *maat* in the eternal cosmos, together with the idea of the deceased's resurrection. Thus, tomb paintings created a specific universe within the tomb, with these images being interpreted on many levels. By hunting wild animals or taming the chaotic forces of nature, the tomb-owner was contributing to the establishment of order. Scenes of agriculture can be viewed on one level as food production with the food nourishing the deceased for eternity and thus ensuring his continuing life in the Afterworld. On another level, the agricultural cycle of seeds, growth and harvest can also be read as a promise of creation, death and resurrection. Flowers, such as the blue lotus, frequently appear in tomb decoration, not only because they were beautiful flowers common in Egypt but also because they symbolized resurrection. The blue lotus starts the day below the surface of the water, and, as the sun rises, the lotus rises out of the water and opens up its blossom to the sun. Once the sun has reached its zenith and starts to set, the lotus closes its flower and slowly sinks back into the darkness below the water, to repeat the cycle on the following day. Thus, the lotus and the sun were two very significant symbols of rebirth and resurrection, although they also could be seen merely as natural parts of the Egyptian landscape.

Representations of the maintenance of *maat* are especially prominent in royal tombs, where the king's chief duty, in death as well
as life, was the establishment and maintenance of *maat*. Thus, in
addition to scenes of the king and the gods, and images of daily
life, royal tomb decoration includes depictions of the king over-
coming his enemies and safeguarding Egypt, or hunting wild
typhonic animals that were the antithesis of *maat* and symbolic of
chaos, disorder and unbalance.

Substructures were not commonly ornamented, although there
are some examples of decorated burial chambers. In the Old
Kingdom some non-royal tombs show offerings and offering lists,
and occasionally scenes of food production. From the end of the
Fifth Dynasty on, royal burial chambers were inscribed with the
Pyramid Texts (Chapter 2), although this practice was abandoned
in the Middle Kingdom for royalty, but was taken over by certain
non-royal individuals of that period, and was commonly used
again by high-status individuals of the Twenty-sixth Dynasty.
New Kingdom royal burial chambers were lavishly decorated: the
tombs of the Valley of the Kings. These tombs create, both archi-
tecturally as well as decoratively, the path from this world to the
Underworld. The illustrations of the Eighteenth Dynasty burial
chambers, until *c.* 1350 BC, depict the book of the Amduat (see
Book of the Amduat, Chapter 2), written out as if a papyrus scroll
had been unrolled along the length of the walls. Some pillars are
adorned with large-scale formal images of the king and deities.
For the remainder of the New Kingdom, more brightly coloured
texts enlivened the royal sepulchres, together with large-scale,
vibrantly coloured images of the king and different deities.

Tomb decoration, of both royal and non-royal tombs, did not
remain static through time, although certain scenes were standard. The decoration of the royal offering places (tomb-
chapels/temples) continued to show the establishment of *maat*
and scenes from the kings' reigns, as well as the royal interaction
with the divine, but, by the New Kingdom, there was a greater
emphasis on the king as god who shared his mortuary temple

*Depictions of industrial activity were commonly part of the tomb's decoration.
Frequently the objects shown being produced were for the tomb, and actual examples
of these would, no doubt, be included in the funerary goods. Here, Mereruka's
(Dynasty VI) jewellers (including dwarfs, who were thought to be skilled jewellers) are
weighing out the precious metals, melting them and working them. The finished
products are displayed on the intermediate register. Saqqara.*

The religious focal point was decorated with rows of offering bringers, especially in the Old and Middle Kingdoms. Ti's estates, personified as women, are bringing the harvests to support his mortuary cult. Saqqara.

with the state god of Egypt, Amun. Thus, the mortuary temples of New Kingdom royalty are dedicated not only to the deceased pharaoh but also to Amun and his family (his consort Mut and their child, Khonsu).

The decoration of non-royal superstructures remained more constant through the ages, although some scenes were more in vogue at certain times and in specific areas. Thus, scenes of fishing, fowling and hunting (actively maintaining *maat*), as well as food production, are found in Egyptian tombs of all periods. However, Middle Kingdom tomb chapels of Beni Hasan show unusual scenes of wrestling and warfare, which are unique to both the time period and the site. A significant change in decoration starts to come about in the New Kingdom. In the second quarter of the Eighteenth Dynasty, images of the king start appearing in tombs of high-ranking nobles and continue to be a feature of decoration

Wine, like beer, was an important offering. It not only slaked thirst but also altered the drinker's state, which imbued it with religious and magical significance. This scene, from the tomb of Petosiris (Ptolemaic Period), shows a traditional Egyptian wine-making scene, except that it is executed in a mixture of Egyptian and Greek styles. Tuna el-Gebel.

The triumph of order
over chaos was a major
element of tomb
decoration in order to
maintain maat in both
this world and the next.
Mereruka and his
huntsmen battle against
hippopotami, the symbol
of Seth. Saqqara.

for some time. Also, the autobiographical element increases in tomb decoration; the numerous scenes showing specific events of the tomb-owner's life are shown in great detail and explained in the accompanying texts. Thus, the tomb of Rekhmire (Theban Tomb (TT) 100) illustrates events from his career as a vizier, and the accompanying text actually lays out the duties of his office. A more dramatic change in decoration occurs during the course of the Nineteenth Dynasty. There is a marked decrease in scenes of daily life and a marked increase in images showing religious and funerary rituals, divinities and the journey to the Afterworld. Scenes of festivals involving the god Amun and divine kingship, such as the Festival of the Valley, become increasingly the norm, while images of jewellery making and food preparation dwindle noticeably. Tombs of the Third Intermediate Period are remarkable for the relative paucity of their decoration. During this time decoration moved from the tomb to the coffin and funerary goods, with the different funerary books providing the inspiration for the schema of decoration. The tomb-chapels of the Twenty-fifth and Twenty-sixth Dynasties see an increase in daily life scenes, together with more archaic texts decorating the substructures.

Ptolemaic period tombs show scenes of daily life as well as religious texts in their superstructure. The sepulchres of the Graeco-Roman period are decorated with a combination that shows a delightful, albeit at times naive, synthesis of Egyptian and Classical art and religious beliefs. Beings from typical Egyptian funerary art, such as the god Anubis, appear wearing Roman armour and guarding the portals of tombs. The deceased is shown in a toga, flanked by Isis and Nepthys; the divinities are recognizable only because of the emblems that crown their heads.

The choice and placement of decoration

Royal tombs and temples had a formal grammar of ornamentation. There were certain scenes that had to be placed in the temples for the continuation of *maat* and a stable Egypt. The locations of these decorations were also relatively standard: scenes of the pharaoh defending Egypt against her enemies, as well as any other remarkable exploits of the pharaoh, were placed on the exterior of the temple's walls and pylons and in the first court. The remaining interior chambers were decorated with images of the king praising and offering to his fellow divinities, being received and acclaimed by them, and they, in turn, ensuring his long, successful and stable rule. The idea that these images were repositories of potent magic made them crucially important not only for the cult of the king and his continued existence in the Afterlife but also for the continued stability of Egypt and the Egyptian way of life.

Similarly, the burial chambers of the kings, once decorated, also followed rules. Pyramid texts were organized within the burial chamber so that they were accessible to the king at his convenience. They are written on the walls so that the king can access them in the correct order as he emerges from his sarcophagus, and continue out of the main chamber so that the king could continue to use the spells while he ascended and became one with the stars. Thus, when modern-day visitors enter the burial chambers of pyramids, which would have been sealed in antiquity, they read the spells in the reversed order.

The choice and location of scenes in tombs change over time and geographic locations, although there are certain rules that seem to be followed for a large part of Egyptian history. Most non-royal tomb decoration moves from the exterior to the interior offering focus with an increase in sacred imagery. Thus, chambers located away from the main offering place that are closer to the tomb entrance feature scenes of outdoor activities associated with daily life, moving from wild to domesticated environments. As one draws closer to the focal offering point, scenes of technology dominate the walls, and, as one gets to the funerary focus, scenes of mourning, offerings and spells to speed the deceased on his way become prominent. Naturally there are some variations on this general rule depending on the time period and the cemetery, but in general the decorative schemes follow these rules. As one walks

The catacombs at Kom el Shugafa show a combination of Greek and Egyptian funerary and artistic traditions adopted by Egypt's mixed population in the Graeco-Roman period. Alexandria, photograph by J. Swanson.

through the tomb there is a move from the profane world to the sacred plane where the deceased ultimately rests.

Although all tombs are not identically decorated, there were certain standard scenes (e.g. offerings being brought to the deceased) that were included in tombs and were placed in the same general location in most tombs. The scene types and locations did, however, vary depending on the time period and geographic location of the cemetery. For example, scenes of butchered offerings appear in tombs from all periods of Egyptian history. However, their location, and even function, change over time. In the Old Kingdom Memphite cemeteries the offering chapel tended to contain images of animals being butchered prior to being offered to the deceased. This continued into the Middle Kingdom when, as the tombs tended to consist of only one chamber, their images clustered near the offering list. In both the Old and the Middle

Kingdoms these images tend to cluster in the lower registers of a wall. Although New Kingdom tombs also contain butchery scenes, these are radically curtailed and are rarely on the lowest register. These single vignettes tend to be shown as the butchery for the actual funerary offering at the tomb and are thus depicted with the funerary cortege. In some instances there are no butchery scenes, although they are resurrected in the Twenty-fifth and Twenty-sixth Dynasties as an archaistic practice.

Another pair of stock scenes shows the tomb-owner spearing fish and hunting birds in the marshes. This scene appears throughout Egyptian history and in Memphite tombs is located in one of the first chambers that one enters. In Middle Kingdom tombs these scenes tend to be located near doorways, while in the New Kingdom they are generally located in the long hall of the "T" type tomb commonly found at Thebes, although this scene type is less common in the tombs of the New Kingdom than in those of earlier periods. In some instances scenes of hunting in the desert replace the more traditional fishing and fowling scenes as they provide the same function: establishing control over the disorder and chaos of nature.

There were also certain stylistic trends in tomb decoration. Obviously a popular atelier would provide similar scenes for several tombs, so that the tomb-owners could keep up appearances and impress all and sundry in the Afterlife as well as in the present. Emulation was also a form of flattery, and this is seen in tomb decoration with regard to the king. In the New Kingdom there is a marked increase in chariot hunting scenes during the reigns of Thutmose III and his son Amenhotep II. These two pharaohs were renowned for their prowess in the hunting field and were often shown engaged in the pursuit of game. Their loyal followers, who had no doubt also been companions on these hunts, include similar hunting scenes in their tombs. The scenes almost stop completely in Theban tombs after the reigns of these kings.

The degree of free choice a tomb-owner had in choosing the decoration for his tomb, and how the scenes were placed within the tomb, is unclear. As discussed above, certain scenes were standard, as were certain positions for these scenes. However, how did tomb-owners choose the decoration and its location? One possibility is that ateliers had pattern books that showed the different scenes that they were able to produce, i.e. their specific butchery or hunting sequence as opposed to a variant produced by a rival atelier, with prices, and the tomb-owner would choose a set of images which would then be placed in the tomb by the artists, with the approval of the tomb-owner. As yet no pattern books have ever been recovered from ancient Egypt, so this method of tomb decoration remains a theory.

Alternatively, people visited cemeteries (see Chapter 7), and might have liked images that they saw in other people's tombs, and had them included in their own. Certainly this is very possible with the Twenty-sixth Dynasty tombs as many contain copies of tomb scenes from Theban New Kingdom tombs. The Twenty-sixth Dynasty tomb of Ibi (TT 36) at Thebes is a copy of a tomb at Deir el-Gebrawi in Middle Egypt. Evidence for pattern books is better for this period: scenes from Memphite tombs are reproduced in Thebes. Either the tomb-owner saw the scenes in the north and had them included in his tomb in the south or, more likely, artists travelled and sketched scenes that would be potentially useful or interesting. There are also New Kingdom and other examples of provincial tombs having minor variations on scenes found in Thebes, thus suggesting either travelling artists or tomb-owners, who were inspired to emulate the scenes and styles of that more cosmopolitan city. Tomb-owners whose sepulchres contained more major autobiographical components (e.g. Rekhmire, TT 100) clearly exercised a higher degree of control over the choice of decoration that was featured in their tombs, and such tombs contain scenes that are very specific to the individual. The specific individual scenes also decline dramatically from the late New Kingdom onward.

Notes

[1] In the Archaic Period and early Old Kingdom the majority of non-royal tombs were built of mud brick, with only some being constructed of stone. This was no doubt a result of economic and technological considerations, rather than spiritual ones.

[2] The earliest boat-pit was actually found as part of the tomb of a powerful noble buried at Saqqara in the First Dynasty, rather than as part of a royal tomb.

[3] The pyramid shape can have many symbolic meanings: it alludes to the primeval mound, as well as being a manifestation of the sun's rays shining down through clouds. The shape is also inspired by the *benben* stone, a sacred stone kept at the sun temple at Heliopolis, ancient Iunnu.

7
Funerals, mortuary cults, the living and the dead

Once the tomb had been built and the deceased had been successfully mummified, the body was ready for burial and resurrection. The funeral, with its accompanying rituals, was the last step before the deceased could be resurrected and live forever. After that, the spirit of the deceased had to be supported by the mortuary cult, and interactions between the living and the dead could be achieved through a variety of ways.

Funerals

Egyptian funerals were large, elaborate affairs with the funerary procession and a feast, similar to a wake, being of key importance. Funerary processions are pictured on the walls of several tombs, and are alluded to in ancient texts, including a description found in the tomb of Djheuty (TT 110). These large processions must have been quite dramatic and would have provided the deceased with a spectacular memorial before burial. They consisted of offering-bearers carrying the various grave goods, followed by priests, chanting and waving incense burners. The coffin, lying on a sled, was pulled by a pair of oxen, and milk was poured in front of it to make it easier for the sled to move smoothly. A curious object that

The bier and coffin of Tutankhamun shown being dragged toward his tomb (KV 62). In the far left the image of his heir, Ay, dressed as a sem priest officiating at Tutankhamun's funeral, is visible. Valley of the Kings.

forms part of the procession from the Middle Kingdom on is the *tekenu*. In the Middle Kingdom it appears to be a wrapped figure that is either crouching or in the foetal position, with only the head showing. In the New Kingdom the *tekenu* is shown as an entirely wrapped bundle, or with the head and sometimes an arm showing. Its role in the funerary ritual is enigmatic.

Professional mourners surrounded the coffin, crying, ululating, tearing their clothes and covering their heads with dust and ash. Such hired mourners are known in Egypt today. Family members, crying and mourning the deceased, formed a significant part of the funerary cortege. More grave goods and priests would bring up the rear, until the mourners reached the tomb. The grave goods were deposited within the tomb, while the mummy rested without, permitting friends and family members a last look at the deceased.

Special sacred dances were also probably performed as part of the funerary ritual. The most famous of these is the *mww* dance. The

Mourners form a part of Ramose's (Dynasty XVIII, TT 55) funeral. The procession also includes family members, priests and offering bearers. The procession is placed in the tomb-chapel so that the parade moves toward the burial shaft. Sheikh Abd el-Qurna, West Bank, Luxor.

dance is associated with the sacred city of Buto in the Delta, the site of an important shrine. The dancers, wearing tall openwork reed headdresses, go through a ritual dance that will help maintain the deceased's soul in the Hereafter.

Before being interred the mummy had to be reanimated in order to function in the Hereafter. The "Opening of the Mouth" ceremony, *wepet-r* in Egyptian, was the most important funerary ritual in ancient Egypt, and was instrumental in turning the deceased into an *akh*. The ritual was generally carried out by a *sem* priest, wearing a leopard skin. The priest was often a member of the clergy, but could also be the son and heir of the deceased. During the course of the ceremony, in which the different senses were restored to the corpse, implements that recalled those used at birth were used. A key item was the *pesesh-kef* set. It consisted of a flint blade that broadened to a fork at the end, and two sets of small vessels. Models of these are known from Old Kingdom

A pesesh-kef set used in funerary rituals. The knife is flanked by jars that would have contained sacred oils. Metropolitan Museum of Art.

tombs and continue to occur occasionally until the Eighteenth Dynasty. The knife was probably based on one that was used to cut the umbilical cord of the baby. Severing the umbilical cord meant that the child had to use its own senses to survive on earth, just as the reanimation ritual meant that the deceased had to function as an independent being in the Afterlife. The tomb of Tutankhamun contained a bronze *pesesh-kef* knife flanked by shrines containing four faience cups. The latter contained natron and resin, both crucial elements in mummification. The other key props in this ritual are the adze and the foreleg of an ox. The latter came from a sacrificial animal that no doubt provided the funerary meal. The lector priest would recite magical spells and prayers, while touching the mummy's nose, mouth, eyes, ears and chest, thereby restoring its five senses. Once the mummy was reanimated it joined the mourners for one last time in a funerary feast, equivalent to a wake. No doubt many of the fresh food-offerings of the deceased were consumed during the course of this meal, with a share being set aside for the enjoyment of the deceased.

Once the feast was over and the food consumed, the corpse was placed reverentially in the tomb with appropriate rituals and prayers. Well-wishers would place garlands and flowers on the mummy, and many of these have been found lying on the bodies or coffin lids when the tombs were opened. Once the tomb was sealed, the spiritual aspects of the deceased started the journey to the Afterworld. Symbolically, however, the Opening of the Mouth ceremony, and the transfer of the deceased through the tomb, down the shaft and into the burial chamber, was an assertion that he had achieved the kingdom of Osiris and would flourish in Amentet.

Mortuary cults

Building and equipping a tomb were not sufficient to ensure eternal life; a mortuary cult had to be established if the deceased were to enjoy the Afterlife. Thus, in addition to constructing the tomb, it had to be provisioned on a daily basis, and the cult of the deceased celebrated regularly. This meant that most importantly food, as well as other oblations, such as incense, oils and linens, were regularly offered to the deceased. The mortuary cult was kept alive by priests as well as family members. Offerings would be placed on offering tables and in front of false doors, and that is where incense would be burned and prayers to and for the deceased recited. The offering places were either in the tomb-chapel, or conveniently located outside for those who had no time to go in. In addition to the false doors, areas in front of stelae that were placed outside the tomb and that listed the name and titles of the deceased were also used as cult places.

Statues placed in the tomb, either in the *serdab* or in other parts of the tomb, were also focal points for the celebration of the cult of the deceased. These would be vivified by incensing, and the *ka* of the deceased invoked by the priest, after which the priest would recite the requisite prayers and make offerings. In addition, the dead were remembered by giving votive statues to temples so that

The statue of Mereruka in his tomb was a focal point for his mortuary cult. Originally the statue was hidden behind double leaf doors (the pivot points for the door flaps are still visible). The opening and sealing of these doors to the underworld would have been a part of the cult ritual and part of the priest's responsibilities. Saqqara.

the cult of the dead would be celebrated, together with the cult of the god.

Mortuary cults were endowed by the deceased by putting aside some land and its yields for the specific purpose of supporting his funerary cult. This would pay the priests who looked after the tomb and the cult. These mortuary priests, who worked in rotation, were called the *hemu-ka*, or servants of the *ka*. Other priests involved with the mortuary cult were lector priests who read from sacred books, and were called *hery-hebet*, the keepers of the sacred books. Sometimes, especially from the Middle Kingdom onward, priests from local temples would double as mortuary priests. This provided funds for the temple and ensured a steady supply of priests for the tomb.

The priest's duties were not onerous; they included making offerings to the tomb-owner, reciting prayers, keeping the tomb clean and making sure that the burial was not disturbed. On feast days or major religious holidays special prayers were no doubt recited as well as special offerings provided. Some of the main festivals would have been the new year festival, and the Thoth and the Sokar festivals. Priests were probably paid through the offerings. Presumably, many of the offerings for the deceased's soul were just offered to him formally and, after being presented, reverted to the priest. The priest would either consume or otherwise dispose of the offerings as his payment for the caretaking of the tomb and the cult. Texts from some tombs, such as that of Hepdjefa at Asyut in Middle Egypt, minutely explain the sources for the provisioning of his cult and the payment of the funerary priest.

Of course, as time progressed, the deceased's family would doubtless divert the income from the designated fields to some other use, such as their own cults, or for other practical purposes. This is why the magical aspects of tomb decoration and inscription were so important: even if the actual offerings were not given, the ones listed or depicted would be substituted magically, and succour the deceased for eternity. This is why passers-by also played

Sem priests are identifiable by the leopard skins that they wear over their linen kilts. These spotted skins might have alluded to the stars in the night sky or have other associations with the animals. Real skins were not necessarily worn by the priests: from the tomb of Tutankhamun a priestly stole made of linen with the animal's head and markings made of gold has been found. Tomb of Mereruka, Saqqara.

an important role in the cult of the deceased. Inscriptions on tombs invite visitors inside and request that they read the offering inscription and the name of the deceased, thus magically transforming the depicted objects into real offerings in the Afterlife.

The tomb-owner himself was generally responsible for financing his mortuary cult but, if he died before the completion of the tomb and the organization and endowment of his cult, the responsibility fell to his eldest son and other family members. If he had no son, then his daughter would take on the main burden of this responsibility. The provisioning of the tomb was, in fact, a way for the heir to become officially recognized as such. Thus, the heir became recognized not only by providing for the deceased's cult but also for officiating at the funeral itself. Thus Sabni went into the Eastern Desert to retrieve the body of his murdered father and buried him in his tomb with great pomp. By doing so, he was recognized not only as a good and dutiful child but, more importantly, as his father's heir, in terms of property, as well as position. Legal documents from the end of the New Kingdom and later also show how heirs were recognized on the basis of fulfilling filial obligations in terms of burying and provisioning the cult of the deceased. This was even relevant for royalty: as Tutankhamun was childless, Ay, a General who possessed no royal blood, saw to his burial and officiated as his *sem* priest, thus giving him legitimacy to succeed to the throne. Especially for royalty, the role of the son as chief officiant of the funerary cult was linked to the story of Osiris and Horus, where Horus performed the funerary rites for his father, was thus legitimized, and therefore succeeded him to the throne of Egypt.

Offering formulae and recitations

A series of standard offering formulae to be read by priests, family members and passers-by are inscribed on tomb walls, together with the identifying name and titles of the deceased. These provide the tomb-owner with his continuing identity and offerings for it in the Hereafter. The most ancient and common of these offering formulae is the *hetep-di-nisw* formula, translated as "a gift or boon that the king gives". These formulae are found inscribed on lintels, false doors and offering tables, and they all start with the same phrase. They then continue with a fairly standard offering list consisting of a thousand of bread, a thousand of beer, oxen, fowl, linen, natron and all things good and pure. Generally Osiris or Anubis is mentioned during the course of the invocation. Most Egyptologists believe that the roots of the formula's opening, gifts that the king gives, lie in the practices of the reversion of offerings as illustrated by the king's offerings to temples, and thence their reversion to the priests and other temple dependents. However, it is also possible that the origins of the formula lie in ancient times when the king was regarded as the absolute divine owner of everything, and thus any offerings that were made, were made in his name or, indeed, actually originated from his domains. Similarly, as a special favour, the king might also have personally endowed the mortuary cult of a favourite.

Another significant formula, found commonly in the Middle Kingdom, is the so-called Abydos formula. This text, found on stelae, as well as in other locations, stresses the deceased's arrival in the West, rather than material comforts. Help is hoped for in the barque upon which he travels to the Afterworld, offerings (generally unspecified) are hoped for and prayers for his welcome in Abydos by the gods are offered.

These offering formulae stress not only the different offerings and the eternal life that the deceased sought but his name and titles, so that he would be sure to receive the offerings and prayers in Amentet. Further identification and glorification of the deceased was also a part of many of the texts inscribed on tombs. His character was praised: he had never lied, or stolen, or seized goods from widows and orphans. Thus, after being assured of his sterling character (which, once written down and read out, became an absolute truth magically), passers-by would be even more inclined to recite the offering formulae.

Hetep-di-nisw formulae appeared not only on tombs but also on stelae, and showed the traditional prayer, together with an image of the deceased, as shown on the stela of Mereri from Dendera. Glasgow Museum, photograph by A. M. Dodson.

Until the reign of Pepy I (2289–2255 BC; Dynasty VI) the deceased would hail the living, those who were upon the earth, and who passed the tomb, and ask them to recite the offering formula. There is an implication that the visitors are taking on the role of a priest, and perhaps, in doing so, the prayers are proving religiously beneficial to both the deceased and the visitor. During the reign of Pepy I, the tenor of these texts changed somewhat, and the deceased's requests become demands. The deceased indicates that *if* the formulae are recited then they, in their *akh* form, would praise the visitors to the divine king and the Great God and protect the visitors during their visit to the necropolis. This threat was addressed not only to visitors but also to funerary priests. Clearly the priests had not been being responsible and tomb-owners had tried to force them to be so by threats of punishment by divine and demonic forces. Priests were also encouraged to have their children continue to celebrate the cult, and promises of advancement of rank are also made on tomb walls. By the end of the Sixth Dynasty, the dead cease threatening the living if they fail to recite offering formulae, but do promise positive intercession with the gods if the formulae are recited.

Curses

The idea of a "curse of the pharaohs" or the "mummy's curse" has gripped the public's imagination from the nineteenth century onward and sent a thrill of horror down the spine of many a visitor who has entered an ancient Egyptian tomb. Although authors such as Edgar Allen Poe and Arthur Conan Doyle wrote about mummies' curses, the idea of tombs being cursed really entered public consciousness after the discovery of the tomb of Tutankhamun in 1922. With the dramatic death of Lord Carnarvon, the financer of the Tutankhamun excavation, in 1923, and the tales of all the lights of Cairo going out simultaneously (a not uncommon occurrence in 1923) and dogs howling, the curse mania took hold and enjoyed almost as much attention as the discovery itself, if not more. Tutankhamun's curse, however, was fabricated by the media as a way to increase the sales of papers and also, perhaps, to discredit the excavators. There was no truth to the repeated statements that the tomb had a curse inscribed on the walls that had been erased by the archaeologists, or on a now-lost "clay tablet". Nor can any credence be given to the frequent statement that all the people involved with the excavation came to grisly ends; certainly they died, but many of them did so ten to twenty years after the opening of the tomb, and generally as a result of such supernatural causes as old age or all-too-common disease. Howard Carter, the chief archaeologist, died of cancer at the age of 65 in 1939, seventeen years after the opening of the tomb. Perhaps more tellingly, however, Douglas Derry, who dismembered the mummy and might be held to be especially accursed, died three decades later at the age of 87!

There are a limited number of tombs that are inscribed with what might be called curses, but these are far less frequent than one might expect and, for the most part, disappointingly dull. The *mastaba* of Hesi, Sixth Dynasty, from Saqqara, can be loosely translated as saying:

As for anyone who enters this tomb having eaten abominable

things that the spirit detests, or having copulated, I will enter into judgement [against] him with the council of the great god.

The *mastaba* of Khentika called Ikhekhi (Dynasty VI, Saqqara) also is inscribed with a curse:

> All who enter my tomb in an impure state, having eaten abominations ... they shall not be pure to enter into [it] or there will be judgement against them in the Council [of gods] ... I shall seize his neck like a bird ... I shall put fear of myself in him ... so that the living may fear the [beings] who go to the West ...

Many of these curses are very concerned with impure people entering and polluting the tomb. Clearly, the tomb-chapel was a sacred place, and visitors had to be in a ritually pure state to enter. Thus, those who had eaten forbidden food, had sexual relations and not washed themselves subsequently, or were unclean for other ritual reasons were seriously discouraged from entering a tomb. Thus, it is not only those with evil intentions toward the physical tomb, the grave-goods or the tomb-owner himself who are cursed, but ritually impure visitors who desecrate the holiness of the chapel.

Several curses found in tombs from all periods of Egyptian history are more violent and threaten to destroy the *ba* of the interloper, or to seize his neck, and to destroy him. A particularly fierce curse that appears at Giza in the tomb of Petety, an Overseer, and in an even more intense form in his wife's tomb, threatens the violator of the tomb with being attacked by crocodiles and hippopotami in the water, and serpents and scorpions on land.

The tomb of Tefibi (Tomb III, First Intermediate Period) at Asyut also carries inscriptions that threaten anyone who destroys the tomb or carries out a hostile act against it or the statues (living images of the deceased) found within. The evildoers are cursed: his son will not live to inherit, no one will carry out his funerary ceremonies, his spirit will be deprived of libations and offerings and will perish in the Afterworld.

Although most known curses appear in the entryways of tombs, or on their exterior faces, there are also instances of funerary statues that are inscribed with curses. These are often more brutal than those found on tomb walls. A New Kingdom statue of a man called Wersu and his wife, Sit-re, reads:

> Verily anyone who shall violate my corpse in the tomb-pit, who shall drag my statue from my tomb-chapel, he shall be punished by Re, he shall not receive water at the drink stand of Osiris, he shall not bequeath his gods to his children forever ... The *ka* of Re shall punish him ... his soul shall be destroyed forever.[1]

Theft and usurpation

Despite the many curses inscribed on tombs, necropolis guards, priests and elaborate systems of sealing of the tomb, sepulchres continued to be robbed throughout Egyptian history. Regardless of whether grave-goods were placed in the superstructure, or the blocked substructure, or whether false passages and dead ends had been incorporated into the tomb design as was common with Twelfth Dynasty pyramids, thieves continued to operate successfully and the majority of ancient Egyptian tombs were plundered in antiquity. Naturally the prime targets were the wealthiest tombs belonging to the nobility or royalty. By the Twenty-first Dynasty, the tombs of the New Kingdom pharaohs were under such severe threat by tomb robbers that the authorities wrapped the bodies up and moved them and their surviving grave goods to a discreet and inaccessible tomb in the Theban hills (TT 320) where they remained until their discovery in 1871.

The thieves were often those who had helped build the tomb, complete the burial, or were involved in equipping it: certain burial chambers that have been found sealed show signs of robbery – in the extreme, that of Nefermaat at Meidum (Dynasty IV) had been entirely wrecked, and the mummy mutilated. Thus, embalmers pilfered golden amulets or gilded elements prior to burial, as was the case with the mummies of Henttawy and Neset-Iset, whose mummies were missing most of their gold jewellery. Perhaps those responsible for the precious oils and unguents in funerary vessels poured only half measures, keeping the remainder for themselves or to sell.

Papyri[2] recording the trials of tomb robbers provide a vivid description of the events related to the robbery of royal and priestly tombs:

> We found the pyramid of King Sobkemsaf I ... We took our copper tools and forced a way into the pyramid of this king through its innermost part. We found the substructure, and we took our lighted candles in our hands and went down. Then we broke through the blocking that we found at the entrance to his crypt, and found this god lying at the back of his burial place. And we found the burial-place of Queen Nubkhaes, his wife, placed beside him, it being protected and guarded by plaster and enclosed by a stone blocking. This we also broke through, and found her resting there in the same way.

> We opened their sarcophagi and their coffins in which they were, and found the noble mummy of this king equipped with a khepesh-sword; many amulets and jewels were upon his neck, and his mask of gold was upon him. The noble mummy of the king was completely bedecked with gold, and his coffins were adorned with gold and silver inside and out and inlaid with all kinds of precious stones ...[3, 4]

Not only was Sobkemsaf's tomb robbed, but the mummy was burnt, thus destroying the body for eternity and earning the most severe punishment for the thieves. As a result of the theft and desecration, over forty-five people were arrested, tortured, especially by bastinado or the beating of the soles of the feet, and brought to trial. Punishment for tomb robbing was severe: the five cuts that deprived the victim of the nose, the ears, and other major facial features, impalement and the complete erasure of the thief's name, thus expunging all evidence of his existence in this world and the next.

Despite all efforts to prevent tomb robbing, it continued throughout Egyptian history. Robbers desecrated tombs not only for the gold and jewellery that were to be found within, but also for the expensive oils, unguents, wines and other foodstuffs that were buried with the deceased and could be consumed or sold, leaving no evidence behind. Tomb robbing continued into the modern period, especially after the sixteenth century with the advent of European tourism in Egypt. Thereafter, especially from the nineteenth century onward, tomb robbing for anything ancient that could be sold to tourists and collectors became rife.

Tomb owners did not lose their tombs and grave-goods only to robbers. Usurpation or reusing material was also responsible for the desecration of tombs and the loss of the name of the original tomb owner. Although there were several injunctions against this in Egyptian wisdom texts, such as in the *Instructions for Merykare*, it continued to occur in both royal and non-royal contexts. Blocks from the Old Kingdom pyramid temples of Khufu, Khafre and Userkaf were moved to Lisht and used in the structure of the Twelfth Dynasty pyramid of Amenemhat I. This was economical as it obviated the quarrying, transport and dressing of new stone and might also have been thought to confer the blessings of the earlier kings onto the burial of the later ruler. Perhaps the continuum of kingship was being stressed, and the idea that all of the divine kings shared one great soul, so why not also the building materials for the tomb?

Entire tombs that had been abandoned, or were not in active use, were also usurped by individuals. Princess Idut (Dynasty V) took over an earlier *mastaba* in the Unas cemetery, leaving the name of the original owner in only one or two places. This practice was fairly common throughout Egypt, the only evidence being the faint traces of the names and titles of the original tomb owner. In some instances tombs were usurped by family members.

However, in other cases, members of the same profession (for example, temple gardeners) could usurp one another's tombs and thus share in the scheme of decoration. There are several instances in which objects were taken from a tomb and recarved with the new owner's name. This is especially common with statuary where, with the change of a name, the statue takes on a fresh identity. *Shabtis* were also thus treated: a *shabti* of Ramesses II (Nineteenth Dynasty) was adapted for a private burial, probably in the Twenty-first Dynasty. Even coffins were usurped, sometimes with justification, but more often not. If a coffin was being prepared for one person and his close family member predeceased him, the coffin might be re-inscribed for the dead person and the original owner of the coffin would commission a new one. More commonly, coffins from desecrated burials would be completely emptied and repainted to suit the new owner's name, titles and gender.

The living and the dead

In addition to celebrating the cult of the deceased and reciting the funerary formulae when passing a tomb, the living and the dead had other more informal interactions. Images of deceased ancestors (in the shape of mummiform torsos) were erected at tombs and in household shrines so that the mortuary cult could be easily celebrated. As in modern Egypt, family members would regularly go to visit the tombs of their ancestors and picnic in the cemetery. In antiquity, cemeteries that are now in bare and sandy desert were pleasant spots, with their brightly painted tombs and shady gardens. Visits to the tombs emphasized the continuation of a family and provided an opportunity for the visitors to give the deceased family members news of the living. There were special festivals: the "Festival of the Valley" held annually in Thebes was one such festival, and in some of its aspects might be likened to the Mexican Day of the Dead. During this festival the cult-image of the god Amun-Ra visited the mortuary temples of the kings on the western bank of the Nile. The cult-image was the focal point of a large procession which included funerary images of the dead. At the culmination of the feast at Deir el-Bahari they, together with the god, received offerings and the promise of renewal. These graveyard visits provided an opportunity for the living to ask the dead for their supernatural assistance and advice.

Letters to the dead have been recovered from several cemeteries. These are inscribed on papyri, scraps of linen and, more commonly, pottery bowls. The bowls would be filled with an offering, perhaps some delicacy that the deceased was particularly fond of, and the edges inscribed with a request. The spirit would be attracted by the fine offerings and would be appeased by them, and thus more willing to help solve the problem or answer the question that was inscribed on the bowl.

Missives asking for all sorts of assistance have been recovered from cemeteries. A letter, addressed to a father and husband by his wife and children, asks for his help in obtaining justice and wreaking vengeance on someone trying to defraud them of their inheritance. Another one complains of the inconvenience caused by the illness of a sick maidservant, and asks for divine intervention for her cure. The letters ask the intervention not only of the *akh* of the deceased but also, at times, of Osiris and other divinities. This was because the *akh* had access to Osiris and the divine tribunal.

Not all the dead were good, helpful or peaceable. The souls of those who had died naturally, or had drowned and were thus specially blessed (this latter group was called *hesy* or favoured ones in Egyptian), tended to be non-threatening and helpful. However, those who had died an untimely or violent death, or led evil lives that caused their entry to the Hereafter to be barred, could turn into jealous and vengeful beings called *mut*. Murdered individuals could even become demons who would torment the living. Even the spirits of those who had died peacefully could at times become mischievous and difficult *akh*, especially if they had been angered by the neglect of their cult. Several letters to the dead are addressed to *akh* that clearly scare or threaten the living.

Some letters suggest that the misfortunes that the writer was complaining about were caused by one *akh*, and the *akh* of another individual was asked to arbitrate and solve the problem in the Hereafter. Thus, all aspects of the spirit, from a distant, removed being to a benevolent intercessor to a troublesome ghost who haunted graveyards, were represented in ancient Egyptian funerary beliefs.

Notes

[1] Source: Griffith, F.L. 1915. "A new monument from Coptos". *Journal of Egyptian Archaeology* **2**, 5–6.

[2] Papyri Ambras, Leopold II-Amherst, Harris A, and Mayer A and B.

[3] Papyrus Leopold II-Amherst.

[4] Source: Adapted from Ikram, S. and Dodson, A. 1998. *The Mummy in Ancient Egypt*. London: Thames and Hudson.

GLOSSARY

Amentet "The West", the dwelling place of the Dead.

Ammit "The Devourer", the composite crocodile–lion–hippopotamus monster that ate up the parts of the accursed dead in the Judgement Hall of Osiris.

Amun(-Re) Chief god of Thebes and paramount god of Egypt from the New Kingdom onward.

Anubis God of embalming, represented with a jackal's head.

Apis Sacred bull of Memphis, a form of Ptah.

Apopis Snake-enemy of the sun god.

Aten The physical sun, worshipped during the late Eighteenth Dynasty.

Atum Human form of the sun god, Re.

Bitumen Mineral pitch; any natural hydrocarbon.

Box Lower part of a rectangular coffin.

Canopic Of or pertaining to the preservation of the viscera removed from the body in the course of embalming.

Cartonnage   Material made of linen, glue and plaster. Often used to refer to whole body casing.

Coffer   Lower part of a sarcophagus.

Coffin   A container for a body of a type usually intended to lie within a sarcophagus. It may be rectangular or anthropoid, of stone or wood, but will always have a separate lid and box/trough.

Coffin Texts   Texts inscribed on the interior of the coffin to help the deceased reach Amentet.

Duamutef   Mortuary genius and Son of Horus, represented with a jackal head, and associated with the stomach. Under the tutelage of Neith.

Funerary Books   A series of writings that aid the deceased in journeying safely through the Underworld. The Book of Gates, The Book of What is in the Underworld and the Book of the Heavenly Cow are a few such works.

Gesso   Mixture of glue and gypsum plaster used to cover coffins, statues, etc.

Hapy   Mortuary genius and Son of Horus, represented with an ape head, and associated with the lungs. Under the tutelage of Nepthys.

Hathor   Goddess, represented in either human or cow form. Hathor of the Sycamore is her more funerary manifestation.

Heart scarab   Large scarab placed over the mummy's heart, inscribed with a spell to prevent the organ bearing witness against its owner.

Hetep-di-nisw   Funerary formula for the provision of offerings to the deceased.

Horus   Falcon-god of the sky; son of Osiris and embodiment of Egyptian kingship.

Hypogea   An underground chamber or vault.

Imseti   Mortuary genius and Son of Horus, represented with a human head, and associated with the liver. Under the tutelage of Isis.

Imywet   Aspect of Anubis, "Who is in the Embalming House".

Isis   Goddess; sister-wife of Osiris, mother of Horus and protector of Imseti. Usually found on the foot of a coffin.

Khentiamentiu   Ancient god of Abydos and the dead; represented as a dog, but absorbed by Osiris by the end of the Old Kingdom.

Khentysehnetjer   Aspect of Anubis, "Who is Before the Divine Booth".

Khnum   Rom-headed creator god.

Maat   Goddess of cosmic order.

Mastaba   A tomb type, common from the Archaic period onward. The name "mastaba" derives from the Arabic word for mud-brick bench, which it resembles.

Meretseger   Goddess of Western Theban necropolis.

Mummy   Artificially preserved human or animal corpse. The word is derived from the Persian, *mum*, meaning wax or bitumen.

Natron   Combination of sodium carbonate and bicarbonate, used to desiccate and purify corpses. Occurs naturally in Egypt, especially in the Wadi Natrun, 64 km north-west of Cairo.

Nebtadjeser   Aspect of Anubis, "Lord of the Necropolis".

Neith   One of the four tutelary goddesses of the dead; a goddess of warfare and hunting.

Nepthys   Sister of Osiris, Isis and Seth, and wife of the last of these. One of the four tutelary goddesses of the dead, always shown at the head of the corpse.

Nut   Sky goddess often pictured on tomb ceilings and lids of coffins and sarcophagi.

Opening of the Mouth   Ceremony which served to reanimate the corpse.

Osiris   God of the Dead and resurrection, brother-husband of Isis, murdered by his brother Seth and who consequently became the first mummy.

Pyramid Texts   Magical texts inscribed in the burial chambers of pyramids from the end of the Fifth Dynasty onward.

Qebehsenuef   Mortuary genius and Son of Horus, represented with a hawk head, and associated with the intestines. Under the tutelage of Selqet.

Sarcophagus   Rectangular/quasi-rectangular outermost container, intended to hold coffins of a different form or material. It may be composed of stone or wood.

Selqet   One of the four tutelary goddesses; her sacred creature is the scorpion.

Sem Priest   Priest who performs funerary rights clad in leopard skin, notably the Opening of the Mouth. Often the deceased's eldest son.

Serdab   A sealed room in a tomb containing statues. From the Arabic for cellar.

Seth   Brother and murderer of Osiris.

Shabti   Magical servant figure found in tombs from the mid-Middle Kingdom onward. From the middle of the Eighteenth Dynasty large numbers are to be found in a single burial.

Thoth   Ibis-headed secretary of the gods.

Trough   Lower part of an anthropoid coffin.

CHRONOLOGY

Predynastic period

Badarian Culture	5000–4000 BC
Naqada I (Amratian) Culture	4000–3500 BC
Naqada II (Gerzian) Culture	3500–3150 BC
Naqada III Culture	3150–3000 BC

Horus or throne name	Personal name	Regnal dates	Years ruled
Archaic period			
Dynasty I			
Horus Narmer			
Horus Aha		3050–	
Horus Djer	Iti		
Horus Djet	Iti		
Horus Den	Semti		
Horus Adjib	Merpibia		

Horus or throne name	Personal name	Regnal dates	Years ruled
Horus Semerkhet	Irinetjer		
Horus Qaa	Qebh	−2813	
Dynasty II			
Horus Hotepsekhemwy	Baunetjer	2813−	
Horus Nebre	Kakau		
Horus Ninetjer	Ninetjer		
?	Weneg		
?	Sened		
Horus Sekhemib/ Seth Peribsen	Perenmaet	−2709	
?	Neferkasokar	2709–2701	8
?	?	2701–2690	11
Horus and Seth Khasekhemwy	Nebwyhetepimyef	2690–2663	27
Old Kingdom			
Dynasty III			
Horus Sanakht	Nebka	2663–2654	19
Horus Netjerkhet	Djoser	2654–2635	9
Horus Sekhemkhet	Djoser-ti	2635–2629	6
Horus Khaba	Teti?	2629–2623	6
Nebkare	Seth?ka	2623–2621	2
Horus Qahedjet?	Huni	2621–2597	24

Horus or throne name	Personal name	Regnal dates	Years ruled
Dynasty IV			
Horus Nebmaet	Senefru	2597–2547	50
Horus Medjedu	Khufu	2547–2524	23
Horus Kheper	Djedefre	2524–2516	8
Horus Userib	Khafre	2516–2493	23
Horus Kakhet	Menkaure	2493–2475	18
Horus Shepseskhet	Shepseskaf	2475–2471	4
Dynasty V			
Horus Irimaet	Userkaf	2471–2464	7
Horus Nebkhau	Sahure	2464–2452	12
Neferirkare	Kakai	2452–2442	10
Shepseskare	Isi	2442–2435	7
Horus Neferkhau	Neferefre	2435–2432	3
Niuserre	Ini	2432–2421	11
Menkauhor	Ikauhor	2421–2413	8
Djedkare	Isesi	2413–2385	28
Horus Wadjtawy	Unas	2385–2355	30
Dynasty VI			
Horus Seheteptawy	Teti	2355–2343	12
Nefersahor/Meryre	Pepy I	2343–2297	46
Merenre	Nemtyemsaf I	2297–2290	7
Neferkare	Pepy II	2290–2196	94
Merenre?	Nemtyemsaf II	2196–2195	1

Horus or throne name	Personal name	Regnal dates	Years ruled
First Intermediate Period			
Dynasties VII/VIII			
Netjerkare	?	2195–	
Menkare	Nitokris		
Neferkare	?		
Neferkare	Neby		
Djedkare	Shemay		
Neferkare	Khendu		
Merenhor	?		
Nikare	?		
Neferkare	Tereru		
Neferkahor	?		
Neferkare	Pepysonbe		
Neferkamin	Anu		
Qakare	Ibi		4
Neferkaure	?		
Neferkauhor	Khuihapy		
Neferirkare	?	–2160	
Dynasties IX/X			
Meryibre	Akhtoy I	2160–	
Neferkare	?		
Wahkare	Akhtoy II		

Horus or throne name	Personal name	Regnal dates	Years ruled
?	Senenen …		
Neferkare	Akhtoy III		
Mery …	Akhtoy IV		
(Various)	(Various)		
?	Meryhathor		
Nebkaure	Akhtoy V		
Merykare	?		
?	?	−2040	
Dynasty XIa			
Horus Tepya	Mentuhotep I	2160–	
Horus Sehertawy	Inyotef I	−2123	
Horus Wahankh	Inyotef II	2123–2074	49
Horus Nakhtnebtepnefer	Inyotef III	2074–2066	8
Middle Kingdom			
Dynasty XIb			
Nebhepetre	Mentuhotep II	2066–2014	52
Sankhkare	Mentuhotep III	2014–2001	13
Nebtawyre	Mentuhotep IV	2001–1994	7
Dynasty XII			
Sehetepibre	Amenemhat I	1994–1964	30
Kheperkare	Senusert I	1974–1929	45
Nubkhaure	Amenemhat II	1932–1896	36
Khakheperre	Senusert II	1900–1880	20

Horus or throne name	Personal name	Regnal dates	Years ruled
Khakaure	Senusert III	1881–1840	41
Nimaetre	Amenemhat III	1842–1794	48
Maekherure	Amenemhat IV	1798–1785	13
Sobkkare	Sobkneferu	1785–1781	4
Dynasty XIII			
Khutawire	Wegaf	1781–	
Sekhemkare	Sonbef		
Nerikare	?Amenemhat V		
Sehetepibre	Qemau		
Sankhibre	Amenemhat VI		
Smenkare	Nebnuni		
Hotepibre	Hornedjhiryotef-sa-Qemau		
Swadjkare	?		
Nedjemibre	?		
Khaankhre	Sobkhotep I		
?	Renisonbe		
Auibre	Hor		
Sedjefakare	Kay-Amenemhat VII		
Sekhemre-khutawi	Amenemhat VIII–Sobkhotep II		
Userkare/Nikhanimaetre	Khendjer		
Smenkhkare	Imyromesha		
Sehotepkare	Inyotef IV		
Sekhemre-swadjtawi	Sobkhotep III		

Horus or throne name	*Personal name*	*Regnal dates*	*Years ruled*
Khasekhemre	Neferhotep I		
?	Sihathor		
Khaneferre	Sobkhotep IV		
Khahetepre	Sobkhotep V		
Wahibre	Iaib		
Merneferre	Ay		
Merhetepre	Sobkhotep VI		
Mersekhemre	Neferhotep		
Merkaure	Sobkhotep VII		
Djedneferre	Dedumose		
Seheqaenre	Sankhptahi		
Swahenre	Senebmiu	−1650	

Second Intermediate Period

Dynasty XV

Maaibre	Sheshi	1650−	
Meruserre	Yakobher		
Seuserenre	Khyan		
Nebkhepeshre/			
Aqenenre/Auserre	Apophis	1585−1545	40
?	Khamudy	1545−1535	

Dynasty XVII

Sekhemre-wahkhau	Rahotep	1650−	
Sekhemre-smentawi	Djehuty		

Horus or throne name	Personal name	Regnal dates	Years ruled
Sankhenre	Mentuhotep VII		
Swedjenre	Nebiriau I		
Neferkare	Nebiriau II		
Sekhemre-shedtawi	Sobkemsaf I		
Sekhemre-wepmaet	Inyotef V		
Nubkheperre	Inyotef VI		
Sekhemre-heruhirmaet	Inyotef VII		
Sekhemre-wadjkhau	Sobkemsaf II		
Senakhtenre	Taa I	–1558	
Seqenenre	Taa II	1558–1553	5
Wadjkheperre	Kamose	1553–1549	4

New Kingdom

Dynasty XVIII

Nebpehtire	Amosis	1549–1524	25
Djeserkare	Amenhotep I	1524–1503	21
Akheperkare	Thutmose I	1503–1491	12
Akheperenre	Thutmose II	1491–1479	12
Menkheper(en)re	Thutmose III	1479–1424	54
(Maetkare	Hatshepsut	1472–1457)	
Akheperure	Amenhotep II	1424–1398	26
Menkheperure	Thutmose IV	1398–1388	10
Nebmaetre	Amenhotep III	1388–1348	40

Horus or throne name	Personal name	Regnal dates	Years ruled
Neferkheperure-waenre	Amenhotep IV/ Akhenaten	1360–1343	17
(Ankhkheperure	Smenkhkare/ Neferneferuaten	1346–1343	3)
Nebkheperre	Tutankhamun	1343–1333	10
Kheperkheperure	Ay	1333–1328	5
Djeserkheperure-setpenre	Horemheb	1328–1298	30
Dynasty XIX			
Menpehtire	Ramesses I	1298–1296	2
Menmaetre	Seti I	1296–1279	17
Usermaetre-setpenre	Ramesses II	1279–1212	67
Benenre	Merenptah	1212–1201	11
Userkheperure	Seti II	1201–1195	6
(Menmire-setpenre	Amenmesse	1200–1196	4)
Sekhaenre/Akheperre	Siptah	1195–1189	6
Sitre-merenamun	Tawosret	1189–1187	2
Dynasty XX			
Userkhaure	Sethnakhte	1187–1185	2
Usermaetre-meryamun	Ramesses III	1185–1153	32
User/Heqamaetre-setpenamun	Ramesses IV	1153–1146	7
Usermaetre-sekheperenre	Ramesses V/ Amenhirkopshef I	1146–1141	5

Horus or throne name	*Personal name*	*Regnal dates*	*Years ruled*
Nebmaetre-meryamun	Ramesses VI/ Amenhirkopshef II	1141–1133	8
Usermaetre-setpenre-meryamun	Ramesses VII/ Itamun	1133–1125	8
Usermaetre-akhenamun	Ramesses VIII/ Sethhirkopshef	1125–1123	2
Neferkare-setpenre	Ramesses IX/ Khaemwaset I	1123–1104	19
Khepermaetre-setpenre	Ramesses X/ Amenhirkopshef III	1104–1094	10
Menmaetre-setpenptah	Ramesses XI/ Khaemwaset II	1094–1064	30
(Hemnetjertepyenamun	Herihor	1075–1069	6)

Third Intermediate Period

Dynasty XXI

Hedjkheperre-setpenre	Smendes	1064–1038	26
Neferkare-heqawaset	Amenemnesu	1038–1034	4
(Kheperkhare-setpenamun	Pinudjem I	1049–1026	23)
Akheperre-setpenamun	Psusennes I	1034–981	53
Usermaetre-setpenamun	Amenemopet	984–974	10
Akheperre-setpenre	Osokhor	974–968	6
Netjerkheperre-meryamun	Siamun	968–948	20
(Tyetkheperure-setpenre	Psusennes II	945–940	5)

Horus or throne name	Personal name	Regnal dates	Years ruled
Dynasty XXII			
Hedjkheperre-setpenre	Shoshenq I	948–927	21
Sekhemkheperre-setpenre	Osorkon I	927–892	35
(Heqakheperre-setpenre	Shoshenq II	895–895)	
Hedjkheperre-setpenre	Takelot I	892–877	15
Usermaetre-setpenamun	Osorkon II	877–838	39
Usermaetre-setpenre	Shoshenq III	838–798	40
Hedjkheperre-setpenre	Shoshenq IV	798–786	12
Usermaetre-setpenamun	Pimay	786–780	6
Akheperre	Shoshenq V	780–743	37
Theban Dynasty XXIII			
Hedjkheperre-setpenamun	Harsiese	867–857	10
Hedjkheperre-setpenre	Takelot II	841–815	26
Usermaetre-setpenamun	Pedubast I	830–805	25
(?	Iuput I	815–813)	
Usermaetre-setpenamun	Osorkon III	796–769	30
Usermaetre	Takelot III	774–759	15
Usermaetre-setpenamun	Rudamun	759–739	20
?	Iny	739–734	5
Neferkare	Peftjauawybast	734–724	10
Dynasty XXIII			
Sehetepibenre	Pedubast II	743–733	10
Akheperre-setpenamun	Osorkon IV	733–715	18

Horus or throne name	Personal name	Regnal dates	Years ruled
Dynasty XXIV			
Shepsesre	Tefnakhte	735–727	8
Wahkare	Bokkhoris	727–721	6
Dynasty XXV			
Seneferre	Piye	752–721	30
Neferkare	Shabaka	721–707	14
Djedkare	Shabataka	707–690	16
Khunefertumre	Taharqa	690–664	26
Bakare	Tanutamen	664–656	8
Saite Period			
Dynasty XXVI			
Wahibre	Psammetikhos I	664–610	54
Wehemibre	Nekho II	610–595	15
Neferibre	Psammetikhos II	595–589	6
Haaibre	Apries	589–570	19
Khnemibre	Amasis	570–526	44
Ankhka(en)re	Psammetikhos III	526–525	1
Late Period			
Dynasty XXVII (Persian)			
Mesutire	Kambyses	525–522	3
Setutre	Darius I	521–486	35
?	Xerxes I	486–465	21
?	Artaxerxes I	465–424	41

Horus or throne name	Personal name	Regnal dates	Years ruled
Dynasty XXVIII			
?	Amyrtaios	404–399	5
Dynasty XXIX			
Baenre-merynetjeru	Nepherites I	399–393	6
Usermaetre-setpenptah	Psamuthis	393	1
Khnemmaetre	Akhoris	393–380	13
?	Nepherites II	380	1
Dynasty XXX			
Kheperkare	Nektanebo I	380–362	18
Irimaetenre	Teos	365–360	2
Senedjemibre-setpenanhur	Nektanebo II	360–342	18
Dynasty XXXI (Persian)			
	Artaxerxes III		
	Okhos	342–338	5
	Arses	338–336	2
	Darius III	335–332	3
Hellenistic Period			
Macedonian Dynasty			
Setpenre-meryamun	Alexander (III/I)	332–323	9
Setepkaenre-meryamun	Philippos Arrhidaeos	323–317	5
Haaibre	Alexander (IV/II)	317–310	7

Horus or throne name	Personal name	Regnal dates	Years ruled
Ptolemaic Dynasty			
Setpenre-meryamun	Ptolemy I Soter	310–282	28
Userka(en)re-meryamun	Ptolemy II Philadelphos	285–246	36
Iwaennetjerwysenwy-setpenre-sekhemankhen-amun	Ptolemy III Euergetes I	246–222	24
Iwaennetjerwymenekhwy-setpenptah-userkare-sekhemankhenamun	Ptolemy IV Philopator	222–205	17
Iwaennetjerwy-merwyyot-setpenptah-userkare-sekhemankhenamun	Ptolemy V Epiphanes	205–180	25
Iwaennetjerwyperwy-setpenptahkhepri-irimaetamunre	Ptolemy VI Philometor	180–164	16
Iwaennetjerwyperwy-setpenptah-irimaetre-sekhemankenamun	Ptolemy VIII Euergetes II	170–163	7
	Ptolemy VI (again)	163–145	18
?	Ptolemy VII Neos Philopator	145	1
	Ptolemy VIII (again)	145–116	29
Iwaennetjermenekh-netjeretmerymutesnedjet-setpenptah-merymaetre-sekhemankhamun	Ptolemy IX Soter II	116–110	6

Horus or throne name	Personal name	Regnal dates	Years ruled
Iwaennetjermenekh-netjeretmenekhsatre-setpenptah-irimaetre-senenankhenamun	Ptolemy X Alexander I	110–109	1
	Ptolemy IX (again)	109–107	2
	Ptolemy X (again)	107–88	19
	Ptolemy IX (again)	88–80	8
	Berenike III	80	1
(?	Ptolemy XI	80	1)
Iwaenpanetjerentinehem-setpenptah-merymaetenre-sekhemankhamun	Ptolemy XII Neos Dionysos	80–58	22
-	Ptolemy XII (again)	55–51	4
	Kleopatra VI	58–57	1
(	Berenkike IV	58–55	3)
	Ptolemy XII (again)		
	Kleopatra VII Philopator	51–30	21
(?	Ptolemy XIII	51–57	4)
(?	Ptolemy XIV	47–44	3)
(Iwaenpanetjerentinehem-setpenptah-irimeryre-sekhemankhamun	Ptolemy XV Kaisaros	41–30	11)
Roman period		30 BC–AD 395	
Byzantine period		395–640	

Horus or throne name	Personal name	Regnal dates	Years ruled
Arab period		640–1517	
Ottoman period		1517–1805	
Khedeval period		1805–1914	
British Protectorate		1914–1922	
Monarchy		1922–1953	
Republic		1953–	

FURTHER READING

General works on death

D'Auria, S., Lacovara, P. and Roehrig, C. 1988. *Mummies & Magic: The Funerary Arts of Ancient Egypt*. Boston, MA: Museum of Fine Arts.

Kanawati, N. 2001. *The Tomb and Beyond: Burial Customs of Ancient Egyptian Officials*. Warminster: Aris and Phillips.

Lacovara, P. and Trope, B. T. 2001. *The Realm of Osiris*. Atlanta, GA: Michael Carlos Museum.

Spencer, A. J. 1982. *Death in Ancient Egypt*. Harmondsworth: Penguin.

Taylor, J. H. 2001. *Death and the Afterlife in Ancient Egypt*. London: British Museum.

Chapter 1: The history and land of Egypt

Baines, J. and Málek, J. 1980. *Atlas of Ancient Egypt*. New York and Oxford: Facts on File.

Dodson, A. M. 1995. *Monarchs of the Nile*. London: Rubicon.

Dodson, A. M. 2000. *After the Pyramids*. London: Rubicon.

Kemp, B. J. 1991. *Ancient Egypt: An Anatomy of a Civilisation*. London: Routledge.

Shaw, I. (ed.) 2000. *The Oxford History of Ancient Egypt.* Oxford: Oxford University Press.

Trigger, B. G., Kemp, B. J., O'Connor, D. and Lloyd, A. B. 1983. *Ancient Egypt: A Social History.* Cambridge: Cambridge University Press.

Chapter 2: Beliefs in the Afterlife

Allen, T. G. 1974. *The Book of the Dead, or Going Forth by Day.* Chicago, IL: University of Chicago Press.

Assmann, J. 1989. "Death and initiation in the funerary religion of ancient Egypt". In *Religion and Philosophy in Ancient Egypt.* New Haven, CT: Yale University Press, pp. 135–59.

Faulkner, R. 1969. *The Ancient Egyptian Pyramid Texts.* Oxford: Oxford University Press.

Faulkner, R. 1973–1978. *The Ancient Egyptian Coffin Texts,* vols I–III. Warminster: Aris and Phillips.

Faulkner, R., Goelet, O. and Andrews, C. 1994–1998. *The Egyptian Book of the Dead.* Cairo: American University in Cairo.

Gardiner, A. H. 1935. *The Attitude of the Ancient Egyptians to Death and the Dead.* Cambridge: Cambridge University Press.

Goedicke, H. 1955. "The Egyptian idea of passing from life to death". *Orientalia* **24**: 225–39.

Hornung, E. 1992. *Idea into Image. Essays on Ancient Egyptian Thought* (trans. E. Bredeck). New York: Timken.

Hornung, E. 1999. *The Ancient Egyptian Books of the Afterlife* (trans. D. Lorton). Ithaca, NY: Cornell University Press.

Lesko, L. H. 1977. *The Ancient Egyptian Book of Two Ways.* Berkeley, CA: University of California Press.

Quirke, S. 1992. *Ancient Egyptian Religion.* London: British Museum.

Zabkar, L. V. 1968. *A Study of the Ba Concept in Ancient Egyptian Texts.* Chicago, IL: Chicago University Press.

Zandee, J. 1960. *Death as an Enemy According to Ancient Egyptian Conceptions.* Leiden: Brill.

Chapter 3: Mummification

Adams, B. 1984. *Egyptian Mummies.* Princes Risborough: Shire Publications.

Andrews, C. 1984. *Egyptian Mummies.* London: British Museum.

Brier, B. 1994. *Egyptian Mummies: Unraveling the Secrets of an Ancient Art.* New York: William Morrow.

Caminos, R. A. 1992. "On ancient Egyptian mummy bandages". *Orientalia* **61**: 337–53.

Cockburn, A., Cockburn, E. and Reyman, T. A. (eds) 1998. *Mummies, Disease, and Ancient Cultures.* Cambridge: Cambridge University Press.

Cockburn, T. A., Barroco, R. A., Reyman, T. A. and Pecki, W. A. 1975. "Autopsy of an Egyptian mummy". *Science* **187**: 1155–60.

David, A. R. 1979. *The Manchester Museum Mummy Project.* Manchester: Manchester University Press.

David, A. R. and Tapp, E. (eds) 1984. *Evidence Embalmed.* Manchester: Manchester University Press.

Davies, W. V. and Walker, R. (eds) 1993. *Biological Anthropology and the Study of Ancient Egypt.* London: British Museum.

Edwards, I. E. S. and Shorter, A. W. 1938. *A Handbook to the Egyptian Mummies and Coffins Exhibited in the British Museum.* London: British Museum.

Filer, J. 1995. *Disease.* London: British Museum.

Friedman, R. and Adams, D., (eds) Neckhen News Vol. 9 (Fall 1997) to Vol. 13 (Fall 2001).

Harris, J. E. and Weeks, K. R. 1973. *X-Raying the Pharaohs.* London: Macdonald; New York: Scribners.

Harris, J. E. and Wente, E. F. 1980. *An X-Ray Atlas of the Royal Mummies.* Chicago, IL: Chicago University Press.

Ikram, S. and Dodson, A. 1998. *The Mummy in Ancient Egypt.* London: Thames and Hudson.

Janot, P. 2000. *Les Instruments d'Embaumement de l'Égypte Ancienne.* Cairo: Institut Français d'Archéologie Orientale.

Nunn, J. F. 1996. *Ancient Egyptian Medicine.* London: British Museum.

O'Connor, D., Silverman, D., Fleming, S. and Fishman, B. 1980. *The Egyptian Mummy: Secrets and Science.* Philadelphia, PA: University Museum.

Sauneron, S. 1952. *Le Rituel de l'Embaument: P. Boulaq III.* Cairo: Institut Français d'Archéologie Orientale.

Taylor, J.H. 1995. *Unwrapping a Mummy.* London: British Museum.

Chapter 4: Animal mummies

Gaillard, C. and Daressy, G. 1905. *Catalogue Général des Antiquités Égyptiennes du Musée du Caire: La Faune Momifiée de l'Antique Égypte.* Cairo: Institut Français d'Archéologie Orientale.

Goodman, S. 1987. "Victual Egyptian bird mummies from a presumed late 17th or early 18th Dynasty tomb". *Journal of the Society for the Study of Egyptian Antiquities* **17**(3): 67–77.

Ikram, S. 2000. "The pet gazelle of one of the ladies of the Pinudjem family". *KMT: A Modern Journal of Egyptology* **11**(2): 58–61.

Ikram, S. and Iskander, N. 2002. *Catalogue Général of Egyptian Antiquities in the Cairo Museum: Non-Human Mummies.* Cairo: Supreme Council of Antiquities.

Kessler, D. 1989. *Die Heiligen Tiere und der König.* Wiesbaden: Otto Harrassowitz.

Lortet, L. and Gaillard, C. 1905–1909. *La Faune Momifiée de l'Ancienne Égypte.* Lyon: Faculty of Medicine and Law.

Malek, J. 1993. *The Cat in Ancient Egypt.* London: British Museum.

Martin, G. T. 1981. *The Sacred Animal Necropolis at North Saqqara.* London: Egypt Exploration Society.

Mond, R. and Myers, O. 1934. *The Bucheum,* vols 1 and 2. London: Egypt Exploration Society.

Morrison-Scott, T. C. 1952. "The mummified cats of ancient

Egypt". *Proceedings of the Zoological Society,* London **121**(4): 861–7.

Perizonius, R., Attia, M., Smith, H. and Goudsmit, J. 1993. "Monkey mummies and North Saqqara". *Bulletin of the Egypt Exploration Society* **3**: 31–3.

Sergent, F. 1986. *Momies Bovines de l'Égypte Ancienne.* Paris: l'École Pratique des Hautes Études.

Vos, R. L. 1993. *The Apis Embalming Ritual, P. Vindob.3873.* Leuven: Peeters.

Chapter 5: Funerary equipment and provisioning the dead

Aldred, C. 1971. *Jewels of the Pharaohs.* London: Thames and Hudson.

Andrews, C. 1990. *Ancient Egyptian Jewellery.* London: British Museum.

Andrews, C. 1994. *Amulets of Ancient Egypt.* London: British Museum.

Bierbrier, M. L. (ed.) 1997. *Portraits and Masks: Burial Customs in Roman Egypt.* London: British Museum.

Breasted, J. H., Jr 1948. *Egyptian Servant Statues.* New York: Pantheon.

Brunton, G. 1943. "The bead network of Shashanq Heqa-kheper-re, Tanis". *Annales du Service d'Antiquités de l'Égypte* **42**: 187–91.

Carter, H. and Mace, A. C. 1977. *The Discovery of the Tomb of Tutankhmen.* New York: Dover.

Corcoran, L. H. 1995. *Portrait Mummies from Roman Egypt.* Chicago, IL: Chicago University Press.

Darby, W. J., Ghalioungui, P. and Grivetti, L. 1977. *Food: The Gift of Osiris,* vols 1 and 2. London: Academic.

Dodson, A. 1994. *The Canopic Equipment of the Kings of Egypt.* London: Routledge.

Doxiadis, E. 1995. *The Mysterious Fayum Portraits.* London: Thames and Hudson.

Eaton-Krauss, M. 1993. *The Sarcophagus from the Tomb of Tutankhamun.* Oxford: Griffith Institute.

Edgar, C. C. 1905. *Graeco-Egyptian Coffins, Masks and Portraits.* Cairo: Institut Français d'Archéologie Orientale.

Emery, W. B. 1962. *A Funerary Repast in an Egyptian Tomb of the Archaic Period.* Leiden: Nederlands Instituut voor het Nabije Oosten.

Hayes, W. C. 1935. *Royal Sarcophagi of the XVIII Dynasty.* Princeton, NJ: Princeton University Press.

Ikram, S. 1995. *Choice Cuts: Meat Production in Ancient Egypt.* Leiden: Peeters.

Niwinski, A. 1988. *21st Dynasty Coffins from Thebes.* Mainz am Rhein: Phillip von Zabern.

Parlasca, K. 1966. *Mumienporträta und Verwandte Denkmäler.* Wiesbaden: Franz Steiner.

Petrie, W. M. F. 1935. *Shabtis.* London: British School of Egyptian Archaeology.

Raven, M. 1982. "Corn mummies". *Oudheidkundige Mededelingen uit het Rijksmuseum van Oudheden te Leiden* **63**: 7–38.

Reeves, N. 1990. *The Complete Tutankhamun.* London: Thames and Hudson.

Reisner, G. A. 1967. *Canopics.* Cairo: Institut Français d'Archéologie Orientale.

Schneider, H. D. 1977. *Shabtis,* vols I–III. Leiden: National Museum of Antiquities.

Stewart, H. M. 1995. *Egyptian Shabtis.* Princes Risborough: Shire Publications.

Taylor, J. 1989. *Egyptian Coffins.* Princes Risborough: Shire Publications.

Tooley, A. M. J. 1995. *Egyptian Models and Scenes.* Princes Risborough: Shire Publications.

Walker, S. and Bierbrier, M. L. (eds) 1997. *Ancient Faces: Mummy Portraits from Roman Egypt.* London: British Museum.

Wilkinson, A. 1971. *Ancient Egyptian Jewellery.* London: Methuen.

Willems, H. 1988. *Chests of Life.* Leiden: Ex Orient Lux.

Chapter 6: The tomb

Allen, J. 1994. "Reading a pyramid". In *Hommages à Jean Leclant* (ed. by C. Berger, G. Clerc and N. Grimal). Cairo: Institut Français d'Archéologie Orientale, pp. 5–28.

Arnold, D. 1991. *Building in Egypt.* New York: Oxford University Press.

Cerny, J. 1973. *A Community of Workmen at Thebes in the Ramesside Period.* Cairo: Institut Français d'Archéologie Orientale.

Davies, N. de G. 1943. *The Tomb of Rekh-mi-Reʿ at Thebes.* New York: Metropolitan Museum of Art.

Edwards, I. E. S. 1985. *The Pyramids of Egypt.* Harmondsworth: Penguin.

Garstang, J. 1907. *The Burial Customs of Ancient Egypt.* London: Constable.

Harpur, Y. 1987. *Decoration in Egyptian Tombs of the Old Kingdom.* London: Kegan, Paul, International.

Hodel-Hoenes, S. 2000. *Life and Death in Ancient Egypt* (trans. by D. Warburton). Ithaca, NY: Cornell University Press.

Hornung, E. 1990. *Valley of the Kings: Horizon of Eternity.* New York: Timken.

James, T. G. H. and Apted, M. A. 1953. *The Mastaba of Khentika called Ikhekhi.* London: Egyptian Exploration Society.

Kamrin, J. 1999. *The Cosmos of Khnumhotp II at Beni Hasan.* London: Kegan, Paul, International.

Lehner, M. 1997. *The Complete Pyramids.* London: Thames and Hudson.

Manniche, L. 1987. *City of the Dead: Thebes in Eygpt.* London: Kegan, Paul, International.

Martin, G. T. 1991. *The Hidden Tombs of Memphis.* London: Thames and Hudson.

Nicholson, P. and Shaw, I. 2000. *Ancient Egyptian Materials and Technologies.* Cambridge: Cambridge University Press.

Reeves, C. N. 1990. *Valley of the Kings*. London: Kegan, Paul, International.

Reeves, N. and Wilkinson, R. 1996. *The Complete Valley of the Kings*. London: Thames and Hudson; Cairo: American University in Cairo.

Reisner, G. A. 1936. *The Development of the Egyptian Tomb Down to the Accession of Cheops*. Cambridge, MA: Harvard University Press.

Robins, G. 1997. *The Art of Ancient Egypt*. London: British Museum.

Rossi, C. 2001. "Dimensions and slope in the Nineteenth and Twentieth Dynasty royal tombs". *Journal of Egyptian Archaeology* **87**: 73–80.

Strudwick, N. and Strudwick, H. 1999. *Thebes in Egypt*. Ithaca, NY: Cornell University Press.

Valbelle, D. 1985. *Les Ouvriers de la Tombe: Deir el-Médineh a l'Époque Ramesside*. Cairo: Institut Français d'Archéologie Orientale.

Chapter 7: Funerals, mortuary cults, the living and the dead

Barta, W. 1963. *Die Altägyptische Opferliste von der Frühzeit bis zur Griechisch-Römischen Epoche*. Berlin: Hessling.

Blackman, W. S. 2000. *The Fellahin of Upper Egypt*. Cairo: American University in Cairo.

Borghouts, J. F. 1978. *Ancient Egyptian Magical Texts*. Leiden: Brill.

Davies, N. de G. and Gardiner, A. 1915. *The Tomb of Amenemhet (TT 82)*. London: Egypt Exploration Fund.

Forman, W. and Quirke, S. 1996. *Hieroglyphs and the Afterlife in Ancient Egypt*. Norman, OK: University of Oklahoma Press.

Gardiner, A. 1955. "A unique funerary liturgy". *Journal of Egyptian Archaeology* **41**: 9–17.

Gardiner, A. and Sethe, K. 1928. *Egyptian Letters to the Dead*. London: Egypt Exploration Society.

Garnot, J. 1938. *L'Appel aux Vivants dans les Textes Funéraires Égyptiens des Origines à la Fin de l'Ancien Empire.* Cairo: Institut Français d'Archéologie Oriental.

Goyon, J.-C. 1972. *Rituels Funéraires de l'Ancienne Égypte.* Paris: Cerf.

Janssen, J. J. and Pestman, P. W. 1968. "Burial and inheritance in the community of workmen at Thebes". *Journal of the Economic and Social History of the Orient* **11**: 137–70.

Kanawati, N. and Abder-Raziq, M. 1999. *The Teti Cemetery at Saqqara*, vol. 5. Warminster: Aris and Phillips.

Lexa, F. 1925. *La Magie dans l'Égypte Antique.* Paris: Geuthner.

Lloyd, A. 1989. "Psychology and society in the ancient Egyptian cult of the dead". *Religion and Philosophy in Ancient Egypt.* New Haven, CT: Yale University Press.

Morschauser, S. 1991. *Threat-Formula in Ancient Egypt.* Baltimore, MD: Johns Hopkins University Press.

Peet, T. E. 1930. *The Great Tomb Robberies of the Twentieth Egyptian Dynasty*, 2 volumes. Oxford: Oxford University Press.

Pinch, G. 1994. *Magic in Ancient Egypt.* London: British Museum.

Ritner, R. K. 1993. *The Mechanics of Ancient Egyptian Magical Practice.* Chicago, IL: Oriental Institute/University of Chicago Press.

Roth, A. M. 1992. "The *pss-kf* and the 'Opening of the Mouth': a ritual of birth and rebirth". *Journal of Egyptian Archaeology* **78**: 57–80.

Smith, M. 1993. *The Liturgy of Opening the Mouth for Breathing.* Oxford: Oxford University Press.

Sottas, H. 1913. *La Preservation de la propriété funéraire dans l'ancienne Égypte.* Paris: Champion.

Werbrouck, M. 1938. *Les Pleureuses dans l'Égypte Ancienne.* Brussels: Éditions de la Fondation Égyptologique Reine Elisabeth.

Wilson, J. A. 1944. "Funeral services in the Egyptian Old Kingdom". *Journal of Near Eastern Studies* **3**: 201–18.

INDEX